POETRY
Starting from Scratch

Michael A. Carey

POETRY
Starting from Scratch

A Two Week Lesson Plan
For Teaching Poetry Writing

Michael A. Carey

Foundation Books
Lincoln, Nebraska

POETRY: STARTING FROM SCRATCH.
Copyright © 1989 by Michael A. Carey. All rights reserved.
Printed in the United States of America. No part of this book
may be used or reproduced in any manner whatsoever without
written permission except in the case of brief quotations em-
bodied in critical articles and reviews. For information address
Foundation Books, Inc., P.O. Box 22828, Lincoln, NE
68542 or visit our website at www.foundationbooks.com

Most recent printing designated by the first digit below.
5   6   7   8   9   10

Photo credits: Cover and p. 2 -- Owen Carey

Library of Congress Cataloging-in-Publication Data

Carey, Michael A., 1954-
    Poetry : starting from scratch.

    Includes indexes.
    1. Poetry--Authorship. 2. Poetry--Study and teaching.
I. Title.
PN1059.A9C37   1989   808.1'07   88-82550
ISBN 0-934988-17-X

The paper used in this publication meets the minimum requirements of
American National Standard for Information Sciences - Permanence of
Paper for Printed Library Materials, ANSI Z39.48-1984.

For the purpose of this standard, permanence refers to paper that should
last at least several hundred years without significant deterioration under
normal library use and storage conditions.

For
Dr. Kenneth and Jean Gee
upon whose kitchen table these words were written

Table of Contents

Preface

How do you get children to write? By love--loving to write, loving to read, loving to share what they've written. A child may write persuasively, yet without heart. If a writer wants to move an audience, then the writer has to be moved himself. I'll show you here how to get love into writing.

I'm convinced anyone can become a good, moving writer if he works at it. Children will work if they love what they're doing, if what they're writing matters.

Really, we're always learning to write. When Mary falls off the school swing, she's learning to write. When John is thrust into the role of brother, he looks at his new sister and he is learning to write. He's learning to feel about his world. What John and Mary need next is a little technical help in expressing those feelings. When I hear children on the playground enjoying metaphors and similes--saying what their lunch looked like, or what Mary's hair looks like--then I know I've done my job. They'll continue to grow as writers.

The first job of a creative writing instructor is to inspire and delight. Once you've done that, you won't be able to feed technique fast enough. I seek a relaxed, light-hearted atmosphere the first day. Writing is as different from grammar as riding a horse is from studying his skeleton. Students should feel this festive atmosphere in the classroom.

From now on, normal rules don't apply. This is a new game we play, from a new set of rules. Good humor creates atmosphere. As a visiting writer I'm treated as special, but every teacher, I believe, can create a festive mood: This is a special time. We are creating! Certain stodgy rules are set aside for the moment. We are riding that horse over the landscape, we aren't dissecting his sinews.

Children know if you enjoy writing. You can't fool them, at least not for long. They watch to see if you are doing the exercises. If you write with the assignment, share your work, if you bare your soul as they bare theirs, you've gone a long way toward creating a contagious enthusiasm. Your work and theirs will come alive.

I've tried to keep the flavor of each assignment. I do use different words for different grades, but in this book I've put a seasoning of educational theory, a flour sifter of behavior, and still stay within the measuring cup of the lesson plan. The cups of explanation are heaped near the beginning of the two weeks, and some room is left toward the end where less explanation is needed.

Here, then, is a two-week plan of lessons, starting from scratch, each building on the one that came before. No prior experience is necessary. All you need is a willingness to get into the kitchen, roll up your sleeves and create.

Michael A. Carey
Farragut, Iowa
September 1987

1.
Basic Tools

Dan stares out the window, not hearing a word I say, apparently. The biggest boy, the lowest grades, he catches the teasing. "Dumb Ox," they say. "All brawn and no brain." Dan gains attention by disrupting. He lets me know from the moment I'm introduced. "Poetry is for girls!" he sneers. "It's sissy stuff about flowers and sunshine." He lets me know he wrestles and plays football. "Poetry is boring," he says.

I know right then that Dan can be my greatest ally in the days to come if--and here is the big IF--if I can get him to write and enjoy poetry in the next forty-five minutes. If Dan does it, the rest of the class may scramble to come on stage. Dan might even reconstruct his self-image.

"Dan," I say, "please stand up and go over to the window you like so well. Look out. Don't jump out, just look out."

Dan rises and stares hard at me before going to the window. He is sure this is a reprimand, but not sure what to do about it.

"Name anything you see out there," I say, "anything at all."

"A parking lot," he says abruptly, stretching for the most unpoetic thing he can think of.

"A parking lot," I say. "Very good, Dan. Thank you. You may return to your seat now."

"Can anybody tell me," I ask, "what, inside this classroom, reminds you of a parking lot? It can have one hundred qualities different from a parking lot, as long as it has at least one quality similar to a parking lot."

No answer. Dead silence.
"Well," I say, "what's in a parking lot?"
"Cars," Dan says flatly.
"Right," I say. "And what do you do in a car?"
"You sit in it," Dan says again.
"Exactly! And what happens then?"
"It takes you for a ride!" someone else pipes up.
"Is there anything in this classroom you sit in?"
"Our desks!" everyone shouts.
"What kind of ride does your desk take you on?"
Silence, then, "Through the world of knowledge," "Through childhood!"
We start coming up with easy metaphors like, "Our desks are small wooden cars that take you through a world of knowledge."
I look at Dan and ask if there is anyone who can tell me what in this classroom is like a parking lot?
"I already wrote it," he says. He hands it to me.
I read it out loud: "Our classroom is a parking lot for magical cars that take you for a ride through your imagination."
Everyone applauds and bursts into a frenzy of writing. From that moment on, Dan hasn't a bad word to say and continues to come up with the most fantastic and outrageous images, sparking the more cautious students to take risks. At this point, I am certain the week will go well, thanks to Dan.

CREATE A FESTIVE ATMOSPHERE

The first day I don't have the class do much writing. I like to establish that certain, almost festive, atmosphere, so students know this will not be just English class. It is Creative Writing class. Here the rules are different. I won't be judging them on grammar or spelling, but helping them to think and express themselves creatively. The work has to be fun or else the doors to the rich associative world of the subconscious will not open and the resulting poems will be correct, but bland.
First, we talk about art in general. What is our task as artists? How is writing a poem different from writing a letter? Art, I explain, is short for the word "artificial." Through your chosen medium you are attempting to re-create your feelings

artificially inside someone else. You want your audience to experience your experience. You want them, as T. S. Eliot said, to think your feelings and to feel your thoughts. You want to take your mind, body and soul, to mix and roll them up into a ball and then throw it to your audience where it will explode inside their chests.

SHOW, DON'T TELL

As an artist I don't want to tell you that I am sad. I want you to cry. I want to re-create my sadness in you. If I am happy, I want you to laugh, to have a certain skip in your step after reading my poem. You should see the world differently then, because you would be seeing life's universals through my experience.

In a letter or essay, you **tell** someone **about** something; you are communicating rational thought. Your brain is doing all the work. In art, you want to **show, not tell**. Your heart and mind work together. A comedian doesn't go out to his audience and say, "I heard a funny story the other night. Man you should have been there. It was a riot!" No, he recreates the giddiness he feels inside himself inside of you! When you experience his work you laugh too.

This is the work of an artist, in whatever medium, in whatever emotion.

DO MORE WITH LESS

How does the poet differ from the short story writer? The novelist? Just as a painter uses form, color and lines to re-create his experience, a writer uses words. A novelist has the luxury of more words than a short story writer. The poet hardly gets a drop in the bucket.

The novelist with her hundred or more pages, or even five hundred has the basic tools of plot, dialogue and character. With this palette, she paints the picture of her experience inside the reader. With the magic wand of her pen, she makes it come alive. A short story writer has fewer words. Most well-paying magazines will only take a seven to fourteen page-manuscript. He must do more with less. He doesn't have room for plots and subplots, or many characters. He must condense his message to make five people carry the emotional and intellectual weight of twenty.

The poet must condense language as far as it will go. Most modern poems, (I am generalizing here, as I am throughout) are one to two pages in length. That means, a poet has to say as much, to re-create an experience just as strongly, in one or two pages, as someone else did in five hundred. A novelist may lead up gradually from many scenes and directions before winding up to throw the final punch. Her punch is what I call the artistic impact of the book. It should turn the heads of her audience, so they will see things from a new angle. They should also feel it in their guts. A poet without time to wind up simply jabs out. She is either on target or her whole message is lost.

You inhabit a novel, walk around in it. There are beautiful parts, sad parts, boring parts etc. A poem inhabits you. It either lives there or never gets a chance.

My first rule for beginning poets then is: **Say the most you can in the fewest words.** A perfect poem cannot have another word added to it, without that word being redundant, nor can it bear to lose a word. If I can go up to a student's work and cross out a word and it does not hurt her poem, then I tell her to get rid of it. It does not belong there. It is diluting her work. A poem is like a strong glass of orange juice. If you add three gallons of water, then it will be weak. The more excess you take out the better the taste and the nutrition--the more potent the experience. A poem is like an atom, small but powerful. Bite into it and it explodes inside you with the essence, the perfume. Three quarters of getting published is knowing what to throw away. Knowing what to write is critical, of course, and most people can do that once they learn to open the doors to their subconscious. Knowing how to trim fat is also critical.

Three quarters of my teaching has to do with good editing. Everyone has gems and can write gems. Often, those gems are hidden, buried beneath a clutter of unnecessary words. If I show students how to push away the clutter, they will surprise themselves at how brilliantly their work shines. And they will continue to surprise themselves long after my brief visit.

This concept allows students to accept criticism. If I've marked one poem with more red ink than another poem it may mean I have found more to play with, not that it is a "worse" poem. Students learn to play with their words as if the poem were a jigsaw puzzle. It is just plain fun to move the pieces around and see what happens. There is always more than one way to fit them. It is the task of the artist to find the best way. If the only red marks a student sees are circles over misspellings and poor grammar and points taken off the grade total, then that student may never write creatively. He'll miss the fun in it and see no reason to take risks or make himself emotionally vulnerable. A poem written one day in creative writing class can be taken out the next day in grammar class and "cleaned up," just as a professional writer would before sending it to his publisher. These are two completely different processes and they should be kept separate for the student. In passing, I, as a creative writing instructor, might correct grammar, but never in a way that would be held against them.

START WITH THE BASICS, NOT RHYME

How does a poet say in one or two pages what takes someone else five hundred? How does he recreate more of his experience in less words? What are the major tools of his craft? No matter where I go, or which grade level I am teaching, if I say the word "poetry," most students think "rhyme and rhythm." It is still the first thing that comes to the mind. Rhyme is just one part of the tool: sound. A poem does not have to rhyme to be good. Rhyme is not one of the basic building blocks of good poetry. The danger of starting with rhyme is that most beginning students will find ten rhyming words in a dictionary, stick them at the end of ten lines, and then connect them with anything that comes into their heads. At worst, this is garbage, at best it may be only doggerel. I am more concerned about the slop that connects the rhymes. Rhythm and rhyme take a long time to do well. It is not a starting point. Some students have a natural ear and I will work with them early, but for the great majority of students, a teacher should start with the basics.

MATCH SOUND WITH MEANING

To say more with less you have to speak on more than one level at the same time, learn to speak between the lines. There are many ways to do this. On the first level the immediate concern: What do the words mean? What are you trying to say? The next is the sound of the words. No matter what you think you are saying, you are always also saying something on the subconscious or subliminal level. It is nice to have both levels going in the same direction. You will then double your punch and avoid working against yourself.

SOUNDS

I tell the class to imagine they do not know English and they must try and fathom what I am saying by the tone, the sound of my words. I walk around the class as if it is a prison yard and I am the Gestapo. I point out some poor student as if he is a traitor and utter contemptuously, "Kitten!"

Then, I ask the class what they thought I meant by this. We discuss what the word sounds like.

The harsh "k" and "t's" make it sound hard, ugly, perhaps mean. Yet, "kitten" means something soft and cuddly. Some words connote subconsciously the opposite of what they denote intellectually. I then go up close to a girl in the class as if I am a love-struck Latin lover and say in a tender trembling voice, "Cellar door." The class agrees that, if they did not know English, then they would think I was asking her to marry me, or saying that I loved her. The word "cellar door" (let's think of them as one word) is one of the most beautiful designations in the English language, but it doesn't mean anything beautiful.

If you want to say something tender and loving, you might want to use liquid consonants like: l, f, s, w, h or y and long vowels like $\bar{a}$, $\bar{e}$, $\bar{o}$ or maybe a(hs), or o(ooos). "Sally fell through the willows in the feathery breeze." Even if you did not know English, if you heard that sentence, you would know how I felt about what I was saying.

If you want to say something with conviction, or emphasis; if you want to be didactic, or use a lot of energy, then perhaps you should use short vowels like *i* in pit and harsh consonants like: z, k, t, ch, p, and b. You might want to say something like: "Bobby bashed Billy in the head with a baseball bat." With the accented alliteration of the b's in that sentence you can almost see the bat bouncing on Billy's head.

A writer must remember the variety of ways to say a thing. One way might be right for one poem and wrong for another. One way might be right for one student and wrong for the student sitting next to him. The poem must be consistent within the rules that each poet has created. If you want to go downstairs and kiss Sally as she falls through the willows in the feathery breeze, then go through the "cellar door." If you want to go downstairs to bash Billy in the head with a baseball bat, then you should go through the "basement door." "Cellar door" would be as wrong in the second statement as "basement door" would be in the first.

RHYTHM AND LINE BREAKS

The silence between words is also important in a poem. The beauty of a melody is not simply the notes. It is also the silence between the notes. The notes by themselves would just be noise. The length and intensity of the silence around them helps define the music. The beauty of a flower arrangement is not only the flowers themselves, but the space between the flowers. Likewise, in a poem you can establish a mood by establishing a rhythm between words. You can even change the whole meaning of a poem, or add a new level of meaning by putting silence in the right spot through line breaks.

Let's say I wrote a poem about a pear tree and in that poem I set up a metaphoric relationship between the pear tree and my life. I thought the old tree was dead and dying and here this year, the year I married, it puts out blossoms. I thought I was dying, or my work was dying, but now that I've married, no matter what the future really brings, I feel strong again.

In the first stanza I talk about the tree, in the second I talk about my life and in the last I talk about both. The words I have for the last line of the poem are: "And then the tree breaks into blossom." By cutting that line in two on the word "breaks" I could add a whole new level of meaning into the poem. "And then the tree breaks / into blossom."

By ending on the word, "breaks," I could emphasize it. I could make the reader think for a split second about what a break is. A break on the skin of a branch would be a blemish that might break open later from a bud to a blossom. A break is a wound. If you broke a branch, you would wound the tree. If you broke the tree, you would kill it. A break then, is also a death. With the line, "And then the tree breaks," I would be leaving the reader thinking about blemishes, wounds and death.

But in the next line, the blemish becomes beauty, the wound heals, and from the supposed death comes life. It would be as if I were saying that in order to be reborn, you have first to die, that in order to heal you have first to be wounded, and that in order to be found, you have first to be lost. By breaking the line where I do, I could be saying that the love engendered by my new marriage is such a salvation. The poem then becomes a poem about salvation all because I put silence in the right spot.

COMPARISONS

The two most basic tools for saying more with less, the two most basic building blocks of good poetry writing are, as Dan and his classmates found out earlier, the metaphor and the simile.

Before I am done with them I want the whole class to be able to define and use them appropriately.

"Does anyone know what a metaphor or a simile is?" I ask and am met, usually, by the expected wall of silence. On the board I write:

> metaphor - (lie) (is) -- implied, indirect
> simile -- like, as -- stated, direct
> comparisons

"Can anybody tell me what a comparison is? Metaphors and similes are both types of comparisons. What do you do when you compare things?"

Answers start coming about here. If you compare two things, you might look at one and then the other and see what's similar about them. While you're at it, what's different? That's all you have to be able to do to start writing good poems. Take two things and see what's the same about them, then see what's different about them. If I ask a class to write poems, immediately they freeze up. If I tell them to start by writing a few metaphors and similes, they still freeze up. If I ask them to compare two things, then maybe they'll think about it later. But, if I ask them if they can take any two things in the world and see what's similar and different about them, then of course they can. Young children can.

Simile

Writing a comparison, I emphasize, is like writing an equation. The equals sign is equivalent to the words: "like" and "as." When you **state** a **comparison**, it means you write the equation using the equals sign. Uncle Jimmy is as skinny as a string bean. UJ=SB. This is a simile. An easy way to remember it is the Latin root for *sim* means like. It has the same root, "*similis*," as the word "similar." If you are saying that one thing is similar to something else, then it is a simile.

Metaphor

If you are saying one thing **is** something else, then you are speaking metaphorically. You are substituting one thing for another. A metaphor, then is a substitute -- the Sweet-N-Low of ancient Rome. If you are a substitute teacher, you might be a walking metaphor. Uncle Jimmy **is** a string bean. UJSB. Is Uncle Jimmy really a string bean? Do you really pop off his head and cook him? What you said sounds like a **lie** but it is not really a lie because that is not what you meant and everyone knows it. Everyone knows that you are just **implying** a **comparison** between Uncle Jimmy and the string bean. The weird creature, UJSB, is really an equation. There is an implied equals sign between the J and the S. UJ (=) SB. You just can't see it.

So, a simile is a stated or direct comparison using the words: like or as. A metaphor is an indirect, or implied comparison which does not use the words like or as. More often than not it will use some form of the verb "to be" like "is."

The importance of the metaphor and simile in poetry cannot be over-emphasized. It is at the heart of all creative thinking, whether you are a mechanic, a writer, or a scientist. To put things together that don't normally go together, to see and highlight the connections between things that you don't normally notice, is what creativity is all about. When Einstein wrote: $E=MC2$, he was really writing a simile. He was saying, "Energy is like, it's like. . . mass times the speed of light squared. Yeah, that's the ticket!" He was better at creative thinking than he was at arithmetic.

SIDEWAYS THINKING

Metaphors and similes are good examples of "sideways thinking." What makes creative writing and thinking so scary for a lot of teachers is that they no longer have all the answers. It is the students who have the answers. It is the teachers' job to help them find them.

There are two ways of thinking which should be taught in school: "rational" or "straight line thinking" and "irrational" or "sideways thinking." I will symbolize the first by using a funnel $\lor$. Here, there is one answer and the teacher knows it. You might ask, What is 3+4, 7+0, 6+1?

3+4

7+0

6+1

$\lor$

7

The answer will always be 7. You are teaching students to funnel or channel and departmentalize their thoughts. You memorize facts and retrieve the appropriate data at the appropriate time. It is a very important skill. If you take the funnel and give it legs. $\lor$l, you get an M for Math, which is usually a good place to exercise this way of thinking. It is a great process for getting old answers to old questions. But it is not necessarily a great way for finding new answers and/or new questions.

If we take "irrational" or "sideways thinking" we then have a megaphone effect. Here, the student has the answers--the experience, whatever--that he/she wants to communicate. You, as the teacher, must help him/her discover the many different answers and to use only the right one:

$$7$$
$$\wedge$$
$$3+4$$
$$7+0$$
$$6+1$$

You are expanding thought instead of funneling it. If you put a cross through the megaphone /-\, you get an A for Art. The Arts can and should be an effective tool for teaching creative thinking. Art is not a luxury that maybe we'll get to if we have time or money.

METAPHOR AND SIMILE

Back to the metaphor and simile. It is time to make concrete that which I've been pontificating about in the abstract. First, I stand over one of the girls in the class (I will call her Melissa) and say, "What if I were to say that Melissa is a rose? Is that a metaphor or a simile? Why? Let's double check. Is Melissa really a rose? That's what I said. Are there petals sticking out of her head? Does she have long green limbs stuck into the ground? Every time she takes a shower does she grow an inch? No. You know that that is not what I am really saying. You know that I am actually implying a comparison.

"What's a comparison? That's when you take two things and see what's alike and what's different about them. In a split second your mind does this. How is Melissa like a rose and how is she different? What qualities would a girl have that a flower might have?"

Answers come readily here. Flowers are soft. Maybe Melissa has soft hair, soft skin, a soft voice; maybe she's a soft touch if you ask her for money. A flower is pretty, colorful, fragile and sweet. A girl could be all of these things. Maybe Melissa is tall, thin, growing, in bloom. Maybe she took a bath and put on perfume.

What if you touch the stem of a rose? Ouch! Maybe she's gentle and beautiful and soft, but watch out! Don't get her mad; she's got this thorny side and might hurt you! We do the same thing with a boy. "What if I were to call Roger a bull? What would I really be saying about him?" Such examples are outrageous enough and embarrassing enough to break the ice and yet informative enough to keep the lesson going.

Once students get the hang of the definition, I like to prove to them that what I said is true. These are good tools for saying more with less. I ask them to think of a sentence as a train. My thoughts are the cargo. The words are the cars.

If I say, "Melissa is as pretty as a rose," I am using a lot of cars and what cargo am I carrying? Only the one thought, "She's pretty." But, if I said, "Have you seen Melissa? She's a rose!" Melissa's a rose. That's three words. In those three words, I just said: she's tall, thin, young, growing, in bloom, soft, sweet, but watch out don't get her mad. She might scratch! Look how much more I said with fewer words.

We do many such comparisons together.

"Name something you like."

"Pizza!"

"Name something you don't like."

"Homework!"

If I write that as an equation P=HW, how would you make the P=HW? You could do something to one side of the equation, to the pizza. What could you do to a pizza to make it as awful as homework?

The students might say, "Put anchovies on it!"

How then, could we put homework, pizza and anchovies together in a sentence so that there is a connection between them?

This example came up once in fourth grade where a little girl came up with the metaphor, "Homework is the only anchovy on the pizza of the weekend." She was young, but well on her way to writing poetry.

"Keep going," I say, "I've helped you up till now. Now do some on your own. Write as many as you can, but at least two of each. Compare something small to something big, something far to something near, something at home to something in school, something under your bed to something in the garage, something imaginary to something real, something on the farm to something in town, something underwater to something in outer space and so on. Don't forget to show me how they're different. It should be obvious how they're similar. Don't simply say, 'My brother is a tornado.' Say, 'My brother is a tornado in the house.'

"If you like writing poetry, compare writing poetry to something else you like. Writing poetry is like eating candy at school. If you don't like writing poetry, compare it to something you don't like. Writing poetry is like being kicked in the teeth by your teacher.

"Look at your pencil, your sheet of paper, the back of the person's head sitting in front of you. Is your paper a large heavy snowflake, or is it a small field of snow that will not melt? Are the ruler lines on your paper the fences in a cattle yard where all the animals have been auctioned, or are they an Olympic swimming pool? If you hold the page in front of you, the lines could be blue rain falling. Maybe it is a venetian blind. The spiral might look like barbed wire. The punched holes could be manholes, or eyeholes for a robber's mask. Your pen might be a rocket ship taking you on a journey through your imagination."

Here are some examples, from all grade levels of what students have come up with on their own:

Mike Carey is like a talking windmill.
Red raspberries in the morning sun sparkle like broken glass.
A sleeping child is like the eye of a hurricane.
Happiness makes me feel like I'm wrapped in giggles.
A face is a bulletin board full of messages.
A Snickers bar is a chocolate vacation.
Dandelions are summer's snowflakes.
Joey's hair looks like a brown lawn a gopher got into and then blew up.
A car is a cow that eats gas.
An egg is a tiny shirt for a chicken with too much starch in it. (age 6)
Letting my body sleep is like the restoration of an antique building. (age 82)
The wind is like the sky sneezing.
A cat is a fluffy pillow that walks and meows.

A rainbow is a slide into another world.
Kareem Abdul Jabbar is a toothpick that makes a lot of
  money.
A fire-fly is like a tiny flying flashlight.
Candy is a toy you can eat.
The flag is like the president's pajamas.
A bird is a cloud that sings.
A pregnant woman is a snake with a partly digested
  meal.
Life is a banana split waiting to be eaten.
My fingernails are like sunflower seeds waiting to be
  chewed.
Love is a door anyone can open.
Tina's dimples are like the pits of an apple.
Tina's hair is like the sun at daybreak.
Matt's hair is like a cornfield in the fall.
The plant next to me is like a sad old man in a nursing
  home.
A child in a wheelchair is like a plane with no wings.
My locker is a trash compactor.
Sadness is a droopy cake.
My mother is a rose who has had her petals plucked.
Writing poetry is like running into a guy wire.
My brain is a freezer that needs defrosting.
Love is a wild flower.
Writing poetry is like swallowing a burr bush.

2.
Extending the Metaphor

You can extend a metaphor or simile by simply asking, "What if it were true?"

For instance, one child's metaphor was, "The snow sparkles like diamonds."

I said, "Wow! What if that were really true! What if your mother's earrings were really little snowballs? She'd have to keep them in the ice-box!"

"Yeah!" Sam said, "And when I shovelled snow, I wouldn't have to get paid. In winter we'd all be rich! We'd just scoop up the ground with our shovels and take it to the bank!"

"You've got a poem, Sam," I said. "You've got a poem."

Here are some "What If" poems:

My sister Melissa's hair is really brown spaghetti.
When she needs a haircut, she just gives herself a trim
with her teeth. When she needs a perm,
she curls it with a fork and spoon.
                -- Sara Groves (Kindergarten)

What if
a star were a piece of jewelry?
Astronauts would take laser guns
to cut pieces of the stars.
Astronauts would be
the richest people in the world.
           -- Shane McVay (2nd grade)

What if the moon were cheese?
Everyone would be eating and eating all the cheese!
People would be madly eating all the cheese!
Then, one part of the month, there would be no
   cheese.
People wouldn't eat that part of the month.
Then, when it was time for the moon to come back
people would madly eat the cheese again
and it would go on forever.
           -- Emily Estelle (3rd grade)

If hands were feet, everyone would walk around
doing handstands. At school, all of the students
would write on the floor. Others would take off
their shoes and write with their toes.
           -- Michael A. Carey (with 1st grade class)

If our principal were a snowman
all the classes would be outside
and we'd play all the time.
We'd make lots of Mr. Careys
and take them home to our freezers.
I'd take mine outside every ten minutes.
In the winter, there would be lots of poems.
           -- Sharon Forthum (2nd grade)

(What if a frog were a pencil sharpener?)

Just a Pencil Sharpener?

Forgotten,
a toad-like creature
joined a classroom,
and sat on a shelf.

He munched and crunched
on pencils of all kinds
as the children cranked his tail.
He ate peppermint pencils
day in, day out.

He savored the
red ones the most --
STRAWBERRY!
He also liked
orange and lime.

Finally, one day
he had eaten his last bite --
so full of food.

No matter how hard
the children cranked,
he would eat
no more!

He tried to tell them,
"Just wait a while!"
But, the children were too busy
to listen to a still, small voice.

The children complained to the teacher.
The teacher complained to the principal.
The principal complained to the janitor.

The janitor said to the principal,
who said to the teacher,
who said to the children,
"He'll have to go!"

So, the toad-like creature
was stashed away in a
cool musty room
where he nearly starved --
ALONE,
COLD,
HUNGRY.
He cried softly.

After weeks upon weeks,
suddenly, a streak of light
shone on the floor.
The door cracked open . . .

Reluctantly, a small child walked in.
She went directly to the creature.
She carefully and kindly brushed off the dust
and brought him to a new home
of JOY
HAPPINESS
WARMTH
and most of all . . . PENCILS!
                    -- Charlotte Satre (6th grade)

RIDDLES

In grade school, I give a homework assignment. I ask them to
go home and look at their supper and to describe it in
metaphor, but not to tell us what it really is. Let us try to
guess it the next day in class. This is an old form of poetry
very popular in medieval European courtly life, called the
"Riddle."

In creating the riddle it is great fun to make believe you are the thing you are describing. This is how one extends a metaphor. For instance, one night I had a Reuben sandwich but the restaurant was very stingy with the corned beef so I wrote:

Supper Riddle

I am a red sleeping bag
(corned beef)
camped on a warm snow-covered mountain.
(sauerkraut)
Darkness above.
Darkness below.
(pumpernickel)
I did not see the hole
I was swallowed up in.

(mouth)

One child wrote:

I am a flat red round space station
covered with snow
with little flying saucers
parked on me.
What am I?

(pizza)

Another wrote:

> I am a chubby man's head
> with green hair and
> a brown fluffy hat
> and a moustache
> that goes all the way
> around my head.
> What am I?
>
> (hamburger in bun)

French fries become fingers and planks, spaghetti becomes worms, sauce is blood or lava, mashed potatoes and gravy are volcanoes with brown lava. You can do any kind of riddles: room riddles, animal riddles, food riddles and so on.

Our metaphors can get pretty wild. Afterwards, however, when I hear students in the lunchroom describing their peas as green basketballs, or tater tots as small bales of hay, or that Joey's hair looks like a wheat field after a rain, or Mary's looks like a golden waterfall, then I know that I have done my job. The children are thinking creatively. In the days ahead, when I attempt to channel their feelings into imagery, they will have no trouble coming up with something. The doors have opened.

3.
Dramatic Irony

On the second day and everyday thereafter, I usually read at least a sampling of what was written the day before. This serves as a quick review and gets the students excited about writing again.

If the homework assignment was to write Supper Riddles, then we try to guess them now. Afterwards, I ask if anyone can define or give me an example of a metaphor or simile. By Friday, they're sick of my asking, but everyone usually has it.

What I do next depends on the class and grade level I'm working with. If I'm at the elementary level, or if the students are older but not yet receptive, I continue with the following assignment. It is fun, popular and fairly sure-fire. It does not, however, generate as many quality products (or poems). It is a wonderful little exercise to help establish the process of writing. If things are already moving well along, then I skip to the next more "advanced" assignment.

ORGANIZING PRINCIPLE

Every good poem has its own prosody or organizing principle. No verse is free for the poet who wants to do a good job. I write William Carlos Williams' famous "This Is Just To Say" on the board and we discover the techniques he employs.

This Is Just to Say

I have eaten
the plums
that were in
the icebox

and which
you were probably
saving
for breakfast

Forgive me
they were delicious
so sweet
and so cold
                    -- William Carlos Williams

I recite it twice, then start asking questions. "Who is this poem written to? Where would you find it? What is it saying? What is it imitating?" It is really a poem written to you, the audience, found in a book in the library, but he makes it feel like it is a note to someone else that you accidentally find and read. You might find it on the refrigerator, or in the refrigerator, or on an empty plate, or on a table in front of the refrigerator. (Williams was writing in the early part of the century, so refrigerators, as we know them, were not around yet.)

First, in the note, he confesses to the crime. "Lady, if ya look'n for ya plums, dey ain't there no more. They're all gone! I ate em!"

How do you know that they're not his plums? Williams leaves us certain clues. He says, "You were probably saving for breakfast," but this is inconclusive. Maybe his mother or brother had designs on his plums. Then he says, "Forgive me." He writes a note of apology. He certainly wouldn't have gone to all this trouble if they were his plums to begin with.

In the note then, he says, "I ate the plums; they were not mine; forgive me." He says that he's sorry, but is he really?

How do you know that he is not sorry; that he might do it again if he gets the chance?

In the last stanza, he gives two words about how sorry he is and then spends the rest of the stanza telling how wonderful the "fruits" of his thievery were. To the owner he says, "I'm awfully sorry. I'll never do it again," and to you, his poetic audience, "Ha! Ha! They were great! I'd do it again in a minute!" This is a subtle example of dramatic irony, when the audience knows more than the characters involved in the poem.

IMAGERY

Look how much Williams established in few words! William Carlos Williams helped father modern American poetry. Before he wrote, poets moved from line to line, rhyme to rhyme, and stanza to stanza. Williams generated interest by moving from image to image. He saw the mind working through mental pictures, through the juxtapositioning of images. We dream in images not in written words.

Williams said, "No ideas but in things." Concrete imagery. Lines can be simple and short. When you've established your image or thought you break the line and move. You don't have to finish out any pre-measured number of beats.

"Have you ever," I ask the class, "done anything that you knew was wrong, but you had fun anyway? Have you ever wanted to do something naughty, but never had the courage to? Well, go ahead. Do it right now on paper. I want you to do it and then apologize for it. But, I want to know that you *are not really sorry* through your use of metaphor or simile.

"What was it *like* when you did that thing? Compare something naughty to something good, so your parents will not be mad at you. Prove to them that they are equal. It doesn't have to be true. You can fly to the moon instead of eating supper, become a dinosaur instead of doing your homework; whatever you want."

I then read one I wrote with this exercise. When I taught in Battle Creek, Iowa, a teacher boarded me at her home in Danbury. We rode to school together in her car and then she lent me her car to get around to all the schools. Her husband managed a Ford dealership, so her big white Lincoln

Continental enjoyed good health. It was so tuned up, I never needed to step on the accelerator. Turn the ignition key and POW! I was off and running.

I am exaggerating, but on January ice my stomach tightened as I slid my way into my parking spot both feet firmly planted on the brake. The wheels spun around and around on the ice so much that I sounded like Mario Andretti at the Indianapolis 500. My apology then was tongue-in-cheek hinting that maybe the car could be idled a little slower.

This Is Just to Say

Dear Siobhán,
I am so sorry
your car skidded
around the parking lot
like a huge white
hockey puck. Its sides
dented with each slapshot
from the telephone poles.

If it's any consolation,
I want you to know,
as we headed into
the cement net
of the driveway, most everyone
agreed, the points were
yours and we won.
                    -- Michael A. Carey

I ask the children to pick out the metaphors and similes and to notice how I extended the central simile. I didn't, as we say in the business, mix metaphors. When I started out playing hockey with the car, I didn't switch to baseball in the middle or checkers at the end.

Extend a metaphor by asking, "What if?" What would happen if Siobhán's big white car was really a hockey puck? Well, the telephone poles would become the hockey sticks. Getting it out the driveway without hurting anyone would be like getting the puck into the net and scoring the winning goal. How could Siobhán be angry if her car won the game for us, even though dented as it (imaginatively) was?

A word of caution to the timid. Anything can happen with this assignment. Keep your sense of humor and let them at it. The normal school rules will seem to vanish as, in their minds, they go and do anything that they want. In the process, they learn to like poetry and find it an invigorating experience, both personally and socially rewarding.

One little boy I will never forget, although it was ten years ago in Pennsylvania. Teaching the third grade, I quickly found this child to be the "worst" student in the class. He fidgeted. He threshed around, not sitting still a moment. The teacher would have taken him out of the class, but I insisted he stay.

This little wiggler came up with writing that rocked the class into an explosion of laughter and then inspired them into a fit of scribbling.

> I'm so sorry I stapled
> your parakeet to the wall.
> It had such a beautiful green
> wingspan. It looked like
> a feathery lollipop.

When Nathan Brumbaugh tried it he said:

> Mom, I feel so bad about
> putting the mouse in your bed,
> but seeing your face
> was like watching fireworks
> on the Fourth of July.

Then, a boy who would never really do anything wrong
wrote:

> Mom, I'm so sorry I broke your vase
> but it was like a pile of diamonds
> sparkling in the sun.
> Wow! Now you can take them to the bank!

Finally, we even broke into rhyme:

> Dad, I'm so sorry I shaved the pig
> and gave him your best cologne.
> Now, he smells like Minnie Pearl
> and looks like Sylvester Stallone!

All these were at the third grade level. In fourth and fifth
grades things start getting a little longer and a little more
intricate.

> I am so sorry
> I ate all the
> peanut butter, but
> it smelled so good, I just
> had to eat it.
> Inside, it was like
> going to New York
> with a million dollars
> and having lunch
> with the Statue of Liberty.
> -- Leslie Gilbert (5th grade)

Notice how it was the delightfully unexpected image at the
end that is the charm of this poem. Keep those unexpected
associations coming freely. Ask them to compare. Make
metaphors and similes. What are things *like*?

At the junior high level, the images and connections are longer and more intricate still. I love this one for its imaginative but impeccable logic. How could his mother be mad at him after reading it?

This Is Just to Say

The ball that went through
your window
was a home run.

The World Series
was clinched
by the glass
that shattered.

My wood
pounded the ball
out of the park,
landing in the crowd.

Forgive me
for being Babe Ruth.
You may keep the ball.
I will even autograph it
if you'd like.
          -- Jason Bell (junior high)

   Put together contrasting images. If you compare a rose to a tulip, not as much happens as if you compare a rose to your grandmother. The young student may at first miss excitement by putting too much of the same together. But if that student finds the connection between a rough and a smooth, a wild and a tame, a sweet and a sour or a naughty and nice, then he unexpectedly stumbles into power. The funny poems will be funnier, and the sad ones will be sadder. Images people don't normally put together stimulate creative thinking. The farther the poet makes the audience go to put the images together, the more the audience will appreciate it in the end.

4.
Intimate Conversation

TALKING TO FRIENDS YOU HAVEN'T MET

The poems I like best, speak to me as though the poet is talking to me as my friend. He may have died hundreds of years ago; he is still my friend.

Take an intimate conversational tone rather than one of public pronouncement. A personal poem should also be easier to write. Here's why.

If you ask students to write a poem on a blank sheet of paper, they freeze up. Yet, these same students have no trouble whatsoever talking to their friends -- during class, after class, on the phone. I ask them to think of writing poetry as just talking to a friend they may never meet. Maybe, the poem that they write today will save someone's life one hundred years from now, someone living in this very town, sitting in their very seat. Maybe, their poem will be preserved in a class collection and someone then will read it and say, "This poet knows what I'm going through. She is my friend. She is the only one who really understands."

I ask the class to imagine that they are indeed talking to someone or some thing. I want them to say what they cannot say to his, her, or its face. Maybe you love your mother or grandmother, but you never got around to telling her because it would sound too mushy. Say it to her now on paper. Maybe

there's somebody you don't like. What would you say to her
if you could get away with it?

Maybe you can't talk to that person because she no longer
lives. What would you say to your great-grandparents, or
grandparents, if you could be with them again? What would
you do? Where would you go? What would you ask them?
What would you want to tell them about yourself, your family,
your work? Be specific. Don't tell me what you might say;
actually say it. Remember again the times you went shopping,
walked in the park, washed dishes together. Tell them what
you do now, what it feels like without them here.

What would you say to your future husband, future
children, your dog, your sneaker, a taco, your pencil...? There
is no end of ways to approach the assignment. You can be
funny, sad, angry, loving -- anything. Say what you feel
naturally and compare, compare, compare! See relationships.
The emotional and intellectual weight of the poem should be
carried by the student's use of metaphor and simile.

BE SPECIFIC

Saying, "Grandma, we had great times together," is blah
compared to, "Remember when you held up my feet so I could
climb the apple tree in your yard? And the time I mixed your
potato salad up to my elbows?"

What is a "great time" to one person may be a boring time to
another. To make the great times happen again, we in the
audience must taste them, touch them, feel them, smell them
and see them. Here's how a fifth grader in Clarinda, Iowa,
completed the assignment:

Dear Grandma

Grandma, remember how we used to bake cookies
  together:
peanut butter, oatmeal, chocolate chip?
Remember how we'd steal the chips
before they ever got in the cookies
and they'd melt down our throats
like a chocolate waterfall?
                    -- Regina Wallace (5th grade)

A fifth grade boy in Farragut, Iowa, wrote to his pencil:

Dear Pencil

I wish you'd write
on your own and leave
me alone. You always
get me in trouble.
You write the wrong
answers on my tests;
you write sloppily.
You roll around the floor and make people
trip over you. And
who gets in trouble?
Me, of course.
Mrs. Bredensteiner
never says a word
to you, does she?
That's it Pencil!
Without me, you're
nothing. I think I'll
break you, or sharpen
you down to nothing.
I wish you were
never invented.
                    -- Tim McGargil (5th grade)

A model I use is one I wrote to my mother. In this personal, tender poem, the students recognize I'm taking a risk by opening my life to them. So far, the risk has paid off. From the wild images of the first day, they calm down, searching not only for a metaphor or a simile, but for the *right* metaphor or simile, one appropriate to their emotion.

I explain first, that my mother died in 1975. I hadn't left New Jersey. I hadn't moved to Iowa. I didn't have children, wasn't married, and was definitely not a farmer. So much had happened in my life that I longed to share with my mother. One Christmas, I imagined myself at her grave in New York City.

Graveside: December 1981

Back home, the bins are full
and the tractors shedded.
There is nothing to do
but look for the used equipment
of bankrupt neighbors and the old farmers
who are selling out.

It is unsettling to see them
after so many years, unsatisfied and bitter,
their hardy lives drained into the soil
and nothing to show but debts.
What can the crazy future
hold for us, who know nothing
and are just starting out?

It must sound strange to you
these allusions to husbandry.
When you left us I was single
and had never gone out of New Jersey.

In Iowa, winters are cold.
Frost falls heavily on the branches.
Horses never leave their windbreak.
Still next month, Lord willing,
we will have a baby.
We wanted you to know
we hope it's a girl.

When we left, little angels
were floating from farm to farm
begging for money and singing.
Every daddy was Santa Claus.

Mother,
just this once, we hoped
you would tell us that everything is ok,
that dirt is clean and death is good,
that we are not alone
in our loneliness.

This season
your silence is a grave
that needs constant filling.

We came today to talk to you
and to listen, really praying,
this time, for a miracle,
but all's quiet, all's death,
all's snow.

                    -- Michael A. Carey
                    (for Helen Carey 1925-1975)

After reading the poem we look for the metaphors and
similes. What does it feel like when a farmer has to sell his
farm? What did I mean when I described children caroling as
angelic beggars? What happened to daddies at Christmas
time? Can they imagine a hole inside themselves that stays
empty no matter what you put into it? That's what I'm saying
it feels like when you lose someone you love. I ask them to
listen to the sound of the consonants and vowels especially at
the end of the last stanza.

With each assignment, I read examples of how others--students and teachers--completed the assignment. This helps convince them that poetry is possible, that moving images are within their reach, as near as the nearest pen. Here are a few of my favorite examples with a brief explanation of where they came from.

The first one, a six-year-old boy, wrote during my brief stay in a small town with Iowa's Touring Arts Team. This young man wanted to write a love letter to a girl who did not yet know that she was his girlfriend. He couldn't write yet so I wrote down his words. "What do you want to say?" I asked.

"I don't know!" he replied "You're the poet. You tell me! That's what you're here for!"

"Well," I replied, "in a love poem, a poet usually tells his lover what she is like to him, how he feels about her. Compare her to something different. Be careful, of course. If you compare your girlfriend to a hippopotamus or a rhinoceros, she may get the wrong idea.

"Remember all those metaphors and similes we did, and how we compared things? Let's start with the top and work our way down. What is her hair like?"

"It's black."

"Don't just say black. Black as what?" I asked.

"It's like black . . . silk," he said.

"Ah!" I replied. "Now look at all you've told her. You just said she is soft, classy, beautiful, perhaps even expensive."

"Great!"

"Let's keep going," I said. "What color are her eyes? What do you do when you're together? What does it sound like? How do you feel when you are with her? Don't tell me about it. Make it happen. I want to make believe that I am you."

He simply answered my many questions and I wrote down his answers. This is what we had when we were done:

Dear Rachel

Your hair is like black silk.
I can't remember the color of your eyes
but I know they're as pretty as pearls.
I like playing house with you,
Scott, Nick and Christina,
when I'm the father and you're the mother.

When we put our children to bed
they snore like jackhammers.
When they wake up, we tell them
to go out and play. We sit around
the house then and do nothing.
It's boring, but I like it
because I'm with you.

> Love,
> Ethan
> -- Ethan Sullivan (1st grade)

Bill Broz, an eleventh grade writing instructor in Fairfield, Iowa, wrote this poem to his eleventh grade English teacher of years ago. At Bill's Catholic school in a large city, he had the misfortune to take the course under a coach who reserved his creative skills for sports. His name was Brother Kelly, but his students called him Alvarez Kelly after the famous Mexican outlaw. Allowing students to think and explore for themselves was the last thing in Kelly's mind. The experience left Bill with a determination to teach English, making it exciting and fun.

The Good Padre

Alvarez Kelly,
you little Nazi.
Priest --
           what a joke!
English teacher --
                  what a sacrilege!

You hated
everything I ever
wrote,
read
or
said
in the 11th grade.

Football was all
you loved.
You taught English
like calling plays
out of Warriner's Grammar.
Every move prescribed,
every idea your own.

And you, incapable
of thought,
with nothing
but
pigskin
between your ears.
                  -- William J. Broz

Mr. Broz let a lot out in very few words. Even if he hadn't
told us which sport the good brother coached, we would have
known by his speaking of pigskin. Usually a bad priest
would commit a sacrilege and a bad teacher would be a "joke"
to his students. Here, the poet cleverly inverts this expectation
by saying teaching is a divine calling and failure to teach well
is a sin.

This painfully serious statement couched in irony and humor had an effect on Mr. Broz' class hard to overstate. That their teacher put his true feelings into a poem they could all enjoy, cut my work in half. It was like planting fresh green sprouts into black soil to get living poetry out of them. On the other hand, if a teacher stays aloof from the assignment and only gives negative criticism, buds of enthusiasm wilt and die.

A junior high school girl in Red Oak, Iowa, wrote her poem to me saying she was bored and couldn't think of anything to write. I made everything sound so easy when she knew it was really hard. I told her just to say that on the paper with a metaphor or simile.

Dear Mr. Carey

I've been sitting here forever.
The hands of the clock move slowly,
like an old horse with a heavy load.
I cannot write like you, my teacher.
I cannot rhyme or make words say things
like you can get them to.
My mind is a blank page.
How am I to write as beautifully as you?
That is not possible. You make it sound so easy
that I'm ashamed of anything
I try to do.
                -- Glenna Helms (junior high)

She needn't have been, because she just did it and continued to do it in every poem after.

A third grade teacher wrote this poem. Again, this was not during a classroom experience, but a summer activity with Iowa's Touring Arts Team. These activities were open to the public and my workshops consisted of students from age six to ninety.
Connie had a six-month old boy in her arms and two grade school girls buzzing in for a visit and then blasting off to another workshop. The fact that she could write at all under

such conditions was inspiring to all of us. She said she had never written a poem before, but she wanted to write this one for her great-grandfather, who was the sheriff in Anita, Iowa, at the turn of the century. She never met him but she felt like she had because of the many things he had built that were passed down to her and her growing family. She could still feel the caress of his loving hands, even though so many years separated them.

I asked Connie, "What did he build that has been passed down? Be specific," I went on. Did she know anything else about him?

She said that there were many stories. I asked her to write one down, her favorite. Then Connie and I pared down her story to its essential elements.

She said, "The biggest outlaws my great-grandfather had to deal with during his tenure in office were grave robbers. He wanted to put a stop to grave robbing but he didn't want to get into a life-threatening encounter over dead people.

"One night, Great-grandpa hid out in the cemetery behind a tombstone. About two A.M. the robbers came and started digging up bodies. When they had loaded the bodies and covered them with a tarp, the ghouls walked back to pick up their tools. Great-grandpa snuck up onto the wagon and hid under the tarp.

"As the wagon slowly left the black, black graveyard, Great-grandpa spoke up from under the tarp in a hoarse whisper. 'Where are we going? Take me back! Hurry up! I'm cold. Take me back, I'm cold. I'm cold. I'm cold. Take me back!'

"The robbers were so frightened they ran away leaving all the incriminating evidence behind them. The Anita graveyard never again had a problem with grave robbers."

Well, now Connie had the hand-crafted gifts and the grave robbers story but she didn't know how to end her poem. I reminded her of how we made metaphors and similes by unexpected associations.

We had earlier simply gone to the window, looked out, and made a connection with the first thing that we saw. I told her to try the same thing now. She went to the window and what she saw were Peace Marchers. This was the summer of the Great Peace March across the United States, protesting nuclear

arms. The marchers had spent the night in Anita because of
the beautiful state park.

I said, "Connie, there may be a direct connection between
your great-grandfather and those protesters and that when you
discover it, you could very well have an end to your poem."

She looked skeptical, but she thought about it. When I
returned a few minutes later, Connie had finished her poem.
The connection, like the end to her poem, had been hiding
there all the time. She simply needed to find it. In the future,
when people read her poem, no one will guess the circuitous
route to what would seem like an obvious conclusion.

Dear Great-Grandpa McLaughlin

As you lie at peace beneath the rampant wind,
still in the pine-surrounded cemetery,
I remember how your gifts were yourself:
a deftly built doll cradle, a carved sewing box.
They were hard; they were real; they endured.
Your problem was the graverobbers
who threatened to steal peace from these sleepers.
To protect the cemetery then, you
met their picks and crowbars with humor and won.
Stealing onto the back of their horse-drawn wagon,
you spoke up like an impatient corpse,
startling them and they fled.
As the wind, snow, and rain pit the surface of your
    stone,
I see the peace marchers walking by,
trying to stop the threat of nuclear arms.
Grandfather, you disarmed your enemies once with
    humor.
What jokes can you tell us now?
                    -- Connie Turner (teacher, 3rd grade)

One of the most moving poems I've seen produced with
this exercise came from an eighth grader in Red Oak, Iowa.
She looked like she wasn't even paying attention or liked my
visit. But she wrote--to her father whom she had never met.
He had left her mother before she was born, most likely

because she was being born. She felt, in some way, the awesome guilt for her parents' separation. No word had ever come from him since the day he left -- no cards, no money, nothing. Yet, this mysterious man was her father. What would she like to say to him if she could? This is what she thought she would say:

Dear Dad

What went wrong?
Once you loved my mother,
then something that should
have brightened your days
made you leave as quietly as dusk.

Haven't you wondered
what I look like,
act like,
talk like
or anything about me?

Can you honestly say
that when you left us,
you forgot us?
Doesn't it hurt?

Dad, it's been fourteen years.
If you don't come back soon,
my love will be completely gone.
There is a hole in my heart
with your name written on it.
                    Jennifer P. Nelson (8th grade)

It's obvious, I hope, by now, the variety of material that can come from the same assignment. The examples you choose to read influence the tone of the students' poems. After reading "Graveside," the majority of the students' poems will be serious, tender and loving (but not all). I try to leave the door open to buffoonery, so those who aren't ready to risk becoming emotionally vulnerable can still have fun and write something that they can be proud of.

As the week progresses, I try to open the "serious" door more and close the "wild" one. What attracted them at first can be forgotten as they discover the thrill of the power that they have within themselves, the power to move others to tears and laughter and to share with them their common humanity.

5.
The Senses and Memory

THE FIRST TIME

Today, we start out with mental calisthenics designed to help students root their work in the concrete. Metaphors and similes help a poem take off to a different level of meaning. When students first get the knack of using imagination to see connections, sometimes they go a little overboard. This exercise helps temper that impulse.

This I call my synaesthesia exercise. Synaesthesia is the describing of something through one of your five senses that is usually described through another one of the five senses. It's a mixing up of the senses. "I feel blue." "The light exploded into the room." How can light, something that you see, be described in terms of something that you hear? How can your feelings have a color?

I consider feeling or emotion the writer's sixth sense. "Syn" is short for synthesis or putting together. Again, we are back to putting together things that don't normally go together, unexpected associations. What color is the number 5? What shape is Tuesday? I ask students these questions. As writers they should, at least, have definite opinions on such matters. I have my own theory that this exercise and later assignments tend to support; that every abstraction has concrete qualities. People just can't see them. It is up to the writer to discover them, to make the invisible visible, the abstract concrete, the un-named thing named.

When an audience hears a good metaphor or poem, they say, "Gosh, he hit the nail on the head. It's so clear now, so obvious. Why didn't I say that?" When we say a poem or comparison works, we mean that enough people in the audience agree with the poet's comparison to get the message.

When the first poet got up in the morning and said, "Boy, I feel blue today," his roommate might have said something like "Harry, you're not blue. You're weird. What do you mean you're blue? You're not a Smurf. Don't say crazy things like that. You're starting to frighten me."

Harry, however, was not thinking in straight lines. He was thinking sideways. In the middle of the argument, Harry's roommate probably said, "Hold on a minute. I get it! Say no more."

If Harry wrote out every association inherent in his image, he would have to have used a lot more words. With blue he said a lot in a little. He really said, "If you've got nice red cheeks, good color, then you're probably healthy. If you're healthy, you're probably happy. On the other hand, if you've got no color, if you're pale, or have a bluish tint to your skin from the veins underneath, then you're ill. If you are ill, you're probably depressed. So, if you're blue, then you're depressed."

It sounds long-winded to say it that way, so he just said, "I feel blue," and everyone knew what he meant. Logically it seems not to make sense, but so many people agree with Harry that now, if you're singing a sad song, you're singing the "blues." Is there blue coming out of the singer's mouth? How can a song have a color?

When the bookkeeper says, "We're in the black," he's using synaesthesia, a synthesis of the senses. When a poet does this he is taking something abstract and making it concrete; he is taking something invisible and making it visible. People sometimes think poets are weird. They are not weird. They just think sideways instead of strictly in straight lines.

If the writer wants to re-create his experience inside his audience, then he should help them by making them use all of their senses, the way the writer did when he experienced the original experience. How do we know what is going on around us? We either see it, smell it, taste it, touch it or hear it.

I write these five senses on the board and then add to them the sixth sense of the emotions. To the right of this column I draw two more and label them: #1 and #2.

```
SENSES  #1          #2

Taste
Touch
Sight
Hearing
Smell
Emotions
```

I ask the class to close their eyes and to listen carefully as I am going to make two noises that I want them to describe through their six poetic senses. I want them to find words that incorporate each of the senses and describe accurately the experience that the noise creates inside of them.

I started out by changing the noises for each class in order to get a variety of poems, but later found it more interesting to make the same noises to every class and then compare the results. To my delight, I found that 99 percent of the time, every class used the same words (or close to it).

At this point I can write down ahead of time the exact words that most of the classes will settle on. I tell them that they are learning to describe what is invisible. They are becoming poets.

The first noise is usually a loud sharp slap on the desk. I usually shout, "Bang!" at the same time for amplification. The next is a sweet high squeal,"Weeeeeeeeee!" Here's what a typical result might look like:

SENSES #1		#2
Taste	bitter	lemonade
Touch	hard	soft
Sight	black	yellow/pink
Smell	smoky	lilacs in fresh spring air
Hearing	gun exploding	child on swing
Emotions	startled	happy

I then ask them to use *all* of the words in each column in some descriptive passage: passage #1 and passage #2. They may only use the words from the columns they've written, not the name of the senses themselves: taste, touch, smell, hear, etc. They may write a poem, prose or simply a few sentences. If a particular student doesn't agree with what the class has settled on democratically, then he can change it, but he still has to use the original word somehow.

For instance, if someone did not feel that noise #1 was a gun exploding, he could say, "When the hard black helmets collided, they sounded like a gun exploding." He could write the beginning of a novel:

It was London, 1880, and a fog covered the town. The *smoke* from the chimney mixed with the mist from the sea until all was *black*.

Bitter words flew from the tenement windows, like old clothes, falling to the *hard* cobblestones below. Suddenly, a *gun exploded*. Footsteps receded in the alley behind me. I was scared and *startled* although no one else seemed to notice. I knew then, it was time to call Sherlock Holmes!

Or it can be a finished poem:

> Another *hard* day
> this hot morning.
> *Bitter* coffee
> and *bitter* thoughts
> around the ashtray
> on the kitchen table.
> She was not *startled*
> when her husband left.
> The world simply
> went *black* and painless.
> As she *smoked* cigarette
> after cigarette,
> her heart pounded its fists
> against her ribs
> like a tiny *gun*
> *exploding.*

For "Weeeeee!" one woman came up with:

Unquestioning Love

> We tumbled from the sack swing
> onto the *soft spring*-green grass
> and burst into Grandma's kitchen.
> Her tart *lemonade* drew us
> to the round oak table
> with its fragrant *lilacs.*
> The sleepy-eyed Indian on the blue pitcher smiled
> when she'd slice the lemons and drop them in.
> This was our summer childhood --
> *happy* and unfettered, blooming,
> as everything did,
> in the warmth of Grandma's
> unquestioning love.
>   -- Arleyne Gildersleeve (adult)

They can be short and simple:

Angel

The *child having fun*
rolled toward the *fluffy rose*
in the middle of the *cotton candy cloud.*
She was *pink*
with *happiness.*
                    -- Sharlene Zharne (adult)

Notice the use of synaesthesia at the end of this poem. With this exercise we have forced the reader to use all his senses. We have also forced the writer to write with all of his senses, with his body as well as his mind. Most beginning writers tend to stay with only a couple of the senses, namely, sight and hearing, and their writing is shallow because of it. I remind them always, they should not be describing the noise, but letting the reader *experience* that noise. What did they see, taste, touch, hear, smell, feel when they heard it?

To test how well they did we ask a stranger into the classroom and then see if he or she can match the sound with the right poem. I have never had it fail yet. The students begin to realize then that they are on to something.

After everyone is sharing what they have written we notice how different everyone's is. Although everyone started with the same words, every poem is entirely different. After a while you can even tell who wrote which. Each student has her own voice, his own way of using verbs, her own way of pacing, his own predominant tone.

Sometimes, if we've been together long enough, I give a list of nouns, adjectives and verbs to each student and each writes a poem from these same words. And rarely do we have a problem matching poem with poet after the writing is done. They are beginning to write in recognizable voices.

I try to keep this first exercise to the first fifteen minutes or so of class. It is only an exercise. The students need not try to win the Pulitzer Prize with it or even have a "finished product." It is ok to do things that don't work. Every poem doesn't have to be wonderful. I do not publish every poem that I write, neither did Robert Frost or Yeats.

The students should feel free to try things and fail, to write things that just don't work. That is part of learning to recognize what will work. If a student would write only one good, publishable poem all week, that would be great! If he'd continue to write at that rate, he'd have a book within a year. Most writers would be pleased with that rate of production.

Whether or not a student gets a good poem from this exercise, the next poem will be more rooted because of it. Metaphors and similes make a poem fly and the senses keep it rooted. If a poem can fly without leaving the ground, then you know that your audience will have the courage to take a ride.

MEMORY

Now on to the significant assignment for today which has to do with memory. Writing is physical memory. One hundred years from now what will people know about you, your town, Iowa, the Midwest, love or hate in you, in Iowa in 1989. If you don't write, then everything you are and know, your family, your friends etc. will disappear. The Nazis thought they killed Ann Frank, but she is still alive, talking to us today, because of what she wrote. She was only junior high age and yet, her words are now part of our great literature.

Great literature doesn't come from famous writers sitting in stainless steel towers on either coast. Memorable words come from inside the culture--sensitive people anywhere who remember and write. It comes from doctors (W. C. Williams), insurance men (Wallace Stevens), newspaper men (Mark Twain), farmers (Robert Frost) -- everywhere, from the young and old, city and country. No one can tell your story or the story of those close to you like you can.

In History, there is no such thing as an objective fact. Events happen and then someone writes about them. Do we really know what is happening in Nicaragua or Afghanistan? Have you been there and seen everything that is happening? Of course not. You pick and choose your facts from the reporters that you feel are reliable. History is not necessarily what happened in the past; it is what someone says happened.

true

Once students realize this, then they can begin to realize the power that they have in their own little hands. They have the power, as we all have, to create, maybe even to change, history.

I wrote a poem in an attempt to illustrate this point. As it is popular with the children I visit, I read it .

The poem is called "How Grandma and Grandpa Met." I wrote it after talking to the mother of the "cousin" who taught me how to farm. He had recently died and I wanted to write a poem in his memory. So, I went to his 90-year-old mother, Winnie, and asked her what our farm was like sixty or seventy years ago when her son was growing up there.

"What was the farm like," I asked her later, "when you were a girl, at the turn of the century? How did you meet Wally, your husband?"

Winnie said, "I met my husband at the little Walnut Township one-room school house. We had recently moved fifteen miles from a farm outside Sidney, Iowa, to the Farragut area. Fifteen miles at the turn of the century in rural Iowa was a very long way. There were no roads as there are today. You didn't know anybody who lived at that great a distance.

"As a result," Winnie went on, "I didn't have many friends at my new school. On top of that, I was a shy girl and didn't make friends easily.

"What got my future husband and me together was a box social. All the girls in class made picnic lunches and all the boys bid on them to raise money for some worthwhile project. In this case, not only did the boy with the highest bid get the lunch of his choice, he also got to eat that lunch with the girl who made it. As you might imagine, sometimes the worst looking lunches got the highest bids, depending on who did the cooking.

"Well, as things turned out, no one bid on my lunch. All the other lunches were auctioned off and practically the whole class was outside eating with their sweethearts. I was left all alone--all alone that is, except for one painfully shy boy, lurking in a shadow at the back of the class. He hadn't had the courage to bid on anything. The teacher opened the bidding and he saw that his jig was up. So, without taking his hands out of his pockets, he nodded his head once and we got our first date together.

"Wally and I were both so shy that neither one of us said one word the whole time we were together. We didn't even look at each other. We looked at the food and ate it and then walked to Wally's buggy.

"Well," Winnie continued, "Wally's father had given him an old jalopy of a horse so he wouldn't go hot-rodding around and get into trouble. It was literally on its last legs. It could barely pull Wally and now it had the weight of an extra person in the buggy.

"On top of this," Winnie said, "I lived north of Stony Point, a mile-long incline. Wally lived on the bottom and his horse was not used to climbing hills." Winnie said, "That old horse strained and strained so hard that it passed gas all the way up the hill."

Here were two painfully shy adolescents on their first date, sitting behind a huge rear-end about the size of themselves, and this loud obnoxious thing was happening right in front of them.

She said, "Neither Wally nor I laughed nor said one word."

They tried to ignore it for forty-five long minutes. Neither of them smiled or said one word about it for years afterward.

"Then one day about forty years later," Winnie said, "I heard Wally laughing to himself in the living room. I called and asked him if he was all right.

"He said, 'Winnie, do you remember our first date together? Do you remember Knuckles, my old horse, what he did to us?'"

Finally, they had a good long laugh over their shy beginnings.

I wanted my family--Winnie's family--to have a place in history, to be remembered for something; and who better to represent us than Winnie and Wally? So, I took the major points of the story, condensed them into as few words as possible, and then this message about memory and the importance of writing things down just came out. I did not know what the poem would be about when I sat down to write, I just knew that I would tell Winnie and Wally's story. The poem concerns the horse and what it did, but it is about memory and writing. I tell students that it doesn't matter how crazy or wild or stupid the idea that starts them writing is, if they put their hearts into it, then something good will come from it. Here's what came for me:

How Grandma and Grandpa Met

She was quiet and a good student, so no boy, at first, warmed up to the shy stranger. No one did until the box social. He too was shy and had few friends, so there was no competition to bid him up during the auction. They sat together on the grass for two hours over fried chicken and pickled eggs and some of the sweetest candies he had ever tasted. Not a word was spoken during the meal, after the meal, nor during the auction. A nod of his head was all that was needed to purchase a meal with the girl he desired. On the way home, neither of them laughed when the old horse broke wind loudly, straining by their one-room schoolhouse and all the way up the mile-long incline. All three kept eyes to the ground -- the two lovers, at least, thinking about their meal and the new sweet taste in their mouths. Sixty years later, Grandma let us know and Grandpa publicly laughed, for the first time over their shy beginnings.

Now, all is quiet. Nothing remains -- not the wagon, nor the horse, nor the schoolhouse, nor Grandpa's soft laughter: only this story and just as I've told it.
-- Michael A. Carey (for Winnie Gee)

I ask students to remember the *first time* that they did something, then I ask them to make it come to life.

"Don't just tell me about it; be there again and take me with you. Your first day of school, first bike ride, first basketball game, first kiss, first jaw of tobacco. What's the first Christmas that you can remember? The first birthday? What does Grandma's house taste like on Christmas morning? Use as many of your senses as you can."

How to use all the senses? Now, you don't taste the house, but you might remember tastes you experienced there. Ever wake up to the smell of coffee and bacon and buns in the oven? The little children might squeal with delight as the fire roars above the crackling of paper when they rip into their presents. What does a basketball game taste like? Sound like? Maybe squeaking sneakers. It might taste salty, if you're a player, from the sweat rolling onto your lips. If you're in the stands, it might be salty from popcorn and sweet from Coke.

I wrote the following poem about my first day of kindergarten. I went to a Catholic school in New Jersey. We lived near a perfume plant. The sky smudged pink, night and day. I never saw constellations until I moved to Iowa. The lights from New York City would reflect off the smog and everything would be a bright pink. What did I think?

Think like you did when you were actually living the original experience. The first time I saw a nun up close, I wasn't sure exactly what kind of creature I was dealing with. I thought, maybe, she was some form of horse as she seemed to be wearing blinders. I couldn't see a human feature until I looked directly into her face. The boy next to me in line knew better and tried to prove it to me.

He went right up to Sister Therese and asked politely, "Excuse me, are you a penguin?" He was not being a smart aleck. He was thinking like a child. To a child, such things are possible.

What did I hear? I remember most of the children crying for their mothers, not wanting to be separated. I wanted to go to school. I wanted to be big and smart like my brothers, smart enough to read Bazooka Joe comics that came with our penny bubble gum. I was primed and ready for anyone who could give me such glorious knowledge.

I started having doubts, however, when I saw everyone else so miserable. "Do these children know something that I don't?" I thought. "What are these horses going to do to us once they get us inside where no one can see? Stampede us?"

Grade schools always have a certain smell. I don't know what it is exactly: paper, books, glue . . . The smell I remember most is that of vomit. An unpleasant memory, but if you're asking.

That first week, some of the students stopped crying on the outside, but not on the inside. They were still upset and these "accidents" kept happening. At home, whenever anyone was sick he was usually in bed in his room and my mother took care of it. It was not something we were aware of for very long.

But in school, we had to sit politely with our hands folded on our desks until the janitor came and sprinkled green dust on it. This seemed to me a strange and vulgar ritual to gain passage into adulthood. Now, whenever anyone gets sick, I think of kindergarten.

How did I feel inside? Like most students do, I suppose. Probably the most common simile I get from students, wherever I go, at whatever grade level, is: "School is like a prison." This comparison, usually offered in jest, still has truth in it, even in the best of schools. Children have to give up certain rights. They must come to an institution where they are told what to do.

While the freedom students give up now compares little to the freedom they will gain by applying themselves, still it doesn't necessarily feel that way, especially at first.

I wanted to express this shock of loss, but I didn't want to call school a "prison." The tone of the poem was different. The image I settled on regarded the suits and ties we had to wear from kindergarten through high school. When I put that noose around my neck and that jacket on for the first time, I knew that I would not get them off for at least 13 years. I felt somehow, I was no longer a child. I could no longer flap my wings and fly around like I used to. Here's how these disparate elements fit together:

[handwritten note: without this sentence, this one is not clear.]

Kindergarten

In as much as you can say
New Jersey is beautiful,
it was a beautiful day,
pink, wonderfully pink and starless.

My mother wore a flat cushiony hat
with a bouquet of plastic blossoms
just ready to issue forth
artificial bugs.

The nuns wore blinders,
or so I thought. I heard a faint
neighing from the convent windows.

It wasn't an ugly building
as far as buildings go:
brick, motherless, smelling
of fresh paper and vomit.

Above each doorway
hung a Celtic cross.

Those first lessons were a worthless maze of breath
   and ink,
a waste of energy, the bright faces of the students
   around me.

Above all,
I remember the muffled sobs,
how straight my back felt in its new suit
when I first folded my wings
forever.
                    -- Michael A. Carey

The student should use at least one metaphor or simile and at least four of the six poetic senses. Here's a couple of student examples from different grade levels:

Playing With Nature

It was a hot Friday in May
I was jumping rope with Amy
in the driveway. She was singing,
"Hop, Skip and a Jump" when
Mom called, "Amy! Rachael!
Come in girls!" So we did.
But on the way, in the arms
of the old maple, a yellow
canary sang back to us
and its branches bowed low
like the jump rope.
　　　　　-- Rachael Cobb (4th grade)

Winning Shot

The crowd cheers
like a gust of wind
as I steal the ball
and dribble down
the endless court
in slow motion.
The opposing players
get closer and closer.
As the clock strikes zero,
the ball flies from my fingers
and my soul flies with the ball.
　　　　　-- Tasha Bonnes (7th grade)

Baby Sister

As I held her to me
I could, once again,
smell the first flowers of spring.
Skin as soft as a summer breeze,
her tiny fragile fingers
constantly in motion,
grabbing at the air.
As I held this little miracle
I knew, deep in my heart,
that the love I felt
would go on forever.
                -- Cathy Sands (7th grade)

First Doctor's Office

It was a simple earache.
When he was looking in
I thought he could see my brain.
When he left, I heard birds chirping.
He smiled too much, like a clown.
The nurse was a clown as well.
She told me to roll up my sleeve
while he got a needle and stuck it in me.
When I stopped screaming,
he gave me a piece of candy.
Big deal.
                -- Michael Emerson (8th grade)

First Kiss

Leaning against the
white picket fence,
my heart pounded,
my words faltered.

He stepped closer.
Innocently, I backed away
Snagging the hood of my jacket
on a straying branch.

In childish wonder, we teased
back and forth, back and forth.
And then that touch, like a
dandelion against my cheek.
                    -- Sarah Hennesy (high school)

First Grief

Two cedar trees -- a sorrowing group by the gate.
Why were they sad? I was only three.
Then, the skid came by
bearing a brown baby colt sleeping so beautifully,
still as the earth after a new fallen snow.
                    -- Iowa Andrews (age 82)

All of these poems were written by people who assured me
that they could not write and had never written a poem before.
They almost dared me to get anything out of them. It proves
to me again: You write strongly about what you feel strongly.
Everyone feels strongly about something. I truly believe that
everyone has it in him or her to be a writer. Some work at it
harder and longer.

6.
Vivid Imagery

POEMS FROM PICTURES

This second week of poetry needn't follow the first immediately. Often, I come back months later for a follow-up. This time around, there are no teeth to pull, no walls to knock down. The students know what you're about and feel comfortable with their skills. They want to fly higher and are ready to take guidance. This week students will do without question what they would have thought impossible during the first week.

First, I ask the students to leave their seats and follow me to the library where we find an assortment of art books and sports and nature magazines (any visual imagery that might catch their fancy). They may also bring in pictures from home of themselves, their dogs, their nieces and nephews, cousins, whatever.

The picture can be abstract or realistic as long as it attracts the writer for some reason. I prefer small art prints that can be handled easily, but anything will do. Even though I tell them ahead of time to bring in pictures from home, 90 percent of the students "forget." This is natural and why I am always in cahoots with the school librarian to have a selection of photographs or artwork handy.

After they have all selected their pictures, I ask the students to, "Make believe the picture before you is a screen and your eyes are projectors. A movie is about to unfold on the paper before you. The picture you see is the first frame of that movie."

If a few still balk, I reassure them by pointing out, "You all have already written wonderful poems recreating something from the past. You had to come up with all the imagery yourself. Think how much easier it is now, when all the shapes, colors, people, and places are given to you. Half of your poem is already written. All you have to do is to take the visual imagery and put it into words. Make the picture come to life for those who cannot see it. When people read your poem, they will not see the picture before you. Through your words, they should feel that they too are there, smelling, tasting, touching, seeing, hearing and feeling the world you create. Your pen is the brush and the paper your canvas. Metaphor, simile, synaesthesia and your six senses are your palette."

Then I read them a couple poems that I wrote from pictures which I just happen to have along with me. For the first, I used Charles Wysocki's "Spring in Bloom." It was on a card someone sent to me. I call it an example of neo-American primitive painting because it is painted to look as if the painter was unschooled, although he probably studied for years to get it to look that way. There is a flat two-dimensional quality about the painting. It is realistic and yet there is something unrealistic about it. The weeds in the field are much too big and beautiful. They are also so regular that they look more like a wallpaper pattern than weeds.

"Spring in Bloom" depicts the outskirts of a rural town at the turn of the century. A church stands in the upper right-hand corner and an orchard in the left. At the bottom left, Wysocki has put a farmhouse and on the right, a mill with a paddlewheel. Between the mill and the house a man drives on a dirt road with a horse and buggy.

I made believe that in the wagon, instead of a man, were two school girls, who got out of bed before their parents, stole apples from the orchard and were heading to the mill to press their own stash of cider. Here's how I put these images together:

Early American Small Print Wallpaper

With the trees still shining in dew,
we hitch the horse and wagon

and sneak off to make cider,
hours before our parents awake.

You tell me, once again, how your sister
brought a raccoon to school in her lunchbox.

We laugh over and over, as we play back
in our conversation Miss Miller's reaction.

Bushes dot the landscape like the reoccurring image
of an early American small print wallpaper.

Nothing stirs the air but the tired wings of a few lazy
  flies
already drunk on the juice of our picking.

It is fifty years till your heart attack, so late in life
swooning into the arms of your second husband.

And sixty till my mind fades with the orchard
where future generations have built machine sheds.

Soon, Margery Morrison will run off
with the beautiful sailor who got killed

in the Great War, and come back
but never speak to anyone.

And Billy Stewart will grow fat and have children --
the two things we never thought he'd do.

But what does it matter to us -- young
and bright as the orchard behind us

guiding the horse over the
cinders to the press?

It is still 1915 and the wagon's full of apples.
There is work before us and we are happy.
       -- Michael A. Carey

The second poem mixes this assignment with the memory assignment from the first week. I used a 35 millimeter slide of myself at about age one or two, that my brother had blown up and printed. In it, I am wearing a suit and bow tie because we are visiting my grandmother in Brooklyn. I am surrounded by cement and brick apartments. My aunt, in the background, looks on without smiling. From either side of the picture two hands stick out of suit jacket sleeves and I hold onto them to keep my balance. For some reason, I am pouting. It is a black and white photo, but I remember that the plastic hard hat I am wearing was pink and had two propellers sticking up out of it like antennae. I did not remember the day that the picture was taken so I superimposed over it my earliest memories of moving out of the tenements we used to live in in New York City. I remembered how troubled I was living there and how relieved I was when we left.

Moving

The rattle of the subway
shakes the curb.
In Brooklyn, buildings
are brown
and getting browner. This Saturday afternoon
Aunt Eleanor watches
from a distance,
secretly eating
a candy bar.

Two cars
go whooshing by.
On one
vandals have skewered the antenna
through a potato.

In the playground, gangs
of ten-year-olds
sport home-made
lances,
and stab birds with them, just
to frighten you.

But not today,
not anymore.

Twenty-three years later
you look back
at an old photograph
and remember with what effort
you clung to those two strong
fingers: one your father's
one your uncle's --
who knows, two arms,
anyway, with dark tweed sleeves,
white cuffs
and a hand as big as your head,
ready to walk you
into the air
and out
to the suburbs.

Your mother snaps the picture,
but you are not fooled
by their confidence, their
confederacy
of smiles. You pout your face
and shut your eyes, afraid
of everything,
not wanting to go anywhere,
as they lead
your reluctant little body
snug in its fat
new suit,
and bow tie, and
pink whirlybird
hat.
                    -- Michael A. Carey

The first couple student examples are from the fourth grade level. "Boomtown" is a favorite of mine because Kelly, the young poet, mis-interpreted the photo completely and yet her efforts still resulted in a beautiful poem. Kelly looked at a black and white photograph. It was truly hard to say what it was. Dark gray spread across the bottom of the picture and a light gray lingered at the top. On the horizon, black bumps showed. She assumed it was a picture of a ghost town somewhere in the vast stretches of Wyoming or Colorado. All the images she came up with were dry desert images. When I looked at the caption under the photo, I noticed that the picture was really of the Florida Everglades. Everything she saw was water! Still, the poem is an accurate description of what she saw, of the experience that the photograph triggered inside her.

Boomtown

This world is colorless.
The black trees on the horizon look like a furniture
  store
that has gone out of business.
The tumbleweed rolls over the sandy earth.
The clouds above are desperate for rain.
This land is desperate for rain.
The people who used to live here
look to the heavens for life.
                    -- Kelly Moody (4th grade)

Thinking (from Constable's "Haywain")

A man looking,
What should I do?
On a cart. Water around him.
A silent breeze blowing.
Worrying.

A little cottage empty.
A dog wishing he could swim.
Thinking, "What do I do?"
What does he do?
Thinking about the end.
The end of him and everything.
Think, that's all he can do,
just think.
                    -- Stephanie Catlett (4th grade)

Dancing Flowers

Dancing flowers.
Pretty satin petals
as soft as the snow.
Quiet loudness.
Sh!
                    -- Mary Ann Mayberry (adult)

The Geisha

From before history,
her face existed.
Her blood red lips
and white powdered face.
Her black hair worn up
in her ancient fashion.
She is soft
and smells of roses

like a small, delicate
Japanese doll.
Her dark brown eyes
reach
for happiness and laughter.
Yet, she is sad.
She has searched for something
all these years,
centuries even.
                    -- Sarah Boese (8th grade)

The Night

The moon shone
through the branches
like the sun shining through
the dusty air of an old barn.
The dog sat in the soft grass
by his master,
both listening
to the old rusty windmill
chatter to the cold night air.

They are all alone
as they listen to the night,
the night that is so old.
                    Damon Hickey (7th grade)

Vietnam

The long stalks of elephant grass
slow the pace. They look excited,
like small nervous children wondering
what to do next. But, some inner drive
keeps them going. Knowing
that if they stopped,
Charlie would never let them
see their families and friends again.
They couldn't let their wounded comrades
die in the hands of Charlie.
These men who would give their lives
to protect their homes, their families,
the country that, although
they had no way of knowing,
didn't give a damn.
                        -- Jon Hansen (8th grade)

7.
Poems from Music

By the end of the second week, I hope, the students will realize that anything and everything can trigger a poem. These "assignments" are really gimmicks to get them started: that piece of paper on the ground, that old photograph, a song -- anything has a story to tell. Everything has the whole universe inside of it once you break it open with the force of your imagination.

The results from this day's assignment amazed and delighted me from the first day I tried it. "Abstractions have concrete qualities" is on the right track!

I bring a record player to class, play two songs and then ask the students to write from one of them. I want each student to recreate in his readers what the composer had created in him. If I had asked them to do this the first week, I probably would have been thrown out of the classroom. But, by the second week, they usually give it a try and produce some astonishing results. I remind the students that we have already written poems from one note alone (with the synaesthesia exercise). If they could do that, surely they can write something when I give them a whole song.

I ask the students to close their eyes and listen to song #1 and then song #2. They should jot down any reaction or first impression while the song is playing. Otherwise, they might forget once the second song starts.

It might also be helpful to make a list of the six senses and then find corresponding words that accurately describe the music. They might want to ask themselves some questions.

Where does the music take them? What do they see, smell taste, and so on ? Are they alone or with others? Is it night or day, cold or warm, wet or dry? What time of year is it?

I try to find good songs, new to them, and that are as different from one another as they can possibly be. One of my favorites is Handel's "Solomon's Oratorio" played by a traditional Irish folk group, De Danann. It represents the Queen of Sheba coming home to her king and countrymen. De Danann call it "The Queen of Sheba Comes to Galway." It is a happy festive song. Nine times out of ten, the students' poems from this song will depict some community out celebrating together -- eating, drinking, dancing (which is exactly what Handel had in mind when he wrote it). They rarely pick an Irish community. Usually, it is a traditional American scene, a community like their own, or one of their ethnic background.

Song #2 is "Cafe" by Brazilian guitarist Egberto Gismonti who went into the Amazon jungle and lived for a time, alone, "absorbing" what he experienced. When he went home to the city he put his experience into his music.

After the students "absorb" "Cafe," I have them put their experience into their medium: words. Again, nine times out of ten, I find in the students' work a solitary character, lonely, sad, surrounded by green and, always, water -- an amazingly accurate description of the composer's rain forest surroundings. I don't tell them about the songs until after they've written their poems. When the students realize what they have done, they are quite pleased and eager to go on.

POEMS FROM SONG #1

Bluegrass

Everything is brown, the instruments,
the wall, even the blue jeans
are as brown as the smell
of the brown walls. Behind
the instruments, pale sweaty faces strain,
trying to please their audience.

Everyone is dancing
in this plain room,
everyone but me.

I am standing in the middle
of the dance floor, but
I am only thinking.

The air is as moist as a rosin cube,
waiting for the strings of a bow
to cut into it.

This is not a square dance,
this is a place you go
to wish.
                    -- Jenny Mueller (7th grade)

Country Seasons

The room is as bright
as a jar of fireflies.
A tall man in a straw hat
strums his legs as the
fiddler blows everyone's hearts
from winter into spring.

This old wooden barn
glows, almost, with happiness.
After all the empty years
and dead animals,
it is once again full
of jolly women
and muscular boys
calling to the moon
like bullfrogs in a swamp.

-- Lisa Rubey (8th grade)

POEMS FROM SONG #2

Rainy Day

It is a spring afternoon
and the rain is falling
softly, slowly.
A cool breeze blows
up lazy odors
from the deli below
and the honks of cars
and shouting pedestrians.

From my apartment window
I can see for miles. Everywhere,
there is a feeling of "newness."
The trees are green with buds
and beads of rain dripping
carefully, so as not to break.

But here,
the apartment I live in
is silent and dark.
I am all alone
except for the busy traffic
dirtying the freshly watered streets.
                    -- Jennifer P. Nelson (8th grade)

The Darkening Waters

I am rocking on a cruise
in the middle of the Atlantic,
watching moonlight bounce
off the cresting waves.

At the rail, a strange girl
bows her head, heavy
with sorrow. A song plays
and she cries. No one
sees her but me, by the
green trembling plants.
Inside the dining room,
everyone else in the world
sails on, dancing, singing, eating.
I can smell rain
in the night sky
as the boat, makes it way
through the darkening waters.
            -- Shayne L. Pederson (7th grade)

    What I find most interesting about "Rainy Day" is that
Jenny saw green, regenerative nature from inside the
city. Egberto Gismonti, it seems, was back in a cafe
remembering the forest. The message was totally
communicated invisibly, through art.

8.
Student Reading

Friday should be a day to enjoy what everyone has worked so hard on all week. By now, everyone should have at least one thing he is proud of, even if it is just a metaphor or a simile.

I love it when I am first introduced to a class and they moan and groan and roll their eyes to the ceiling, dreading even the thought of poetry. The teacher, apologetically, wishes me good luck as if I have just accepted the most daring *Mission Impossible* of all time.

Then, on Friday, when I announce that this is our last day together, there are more moans and groans -- but this time, it's because they do not want to stop writing poetry. There is nothing more rewarding than seeing the look in the teacher and students' eyes at that moment. Something magical happens that will outlast my brief visit. A process has begun that will bring others to the appreciation and creation of literature.

All week long, I have been criticizing their work, mostly getting rid of unnecessary words, misleading detail, looking for consistency in tone and sound, looking for an end with a note of finality, or a beginning that leads one on.

As a student finishes writing something good, be it a poem or part of a poem, I read it to the class and discuss what is admirable about it. By the time Friday comes, most of the shyness is gone. I try to catch something wonderful as it is being written and transfer the excitement I feel to the author by reading it back to him with feeling. He is usually a bit taken aback that something so pleasing and effective has come from his pen.

I ask him right then if I can read it to the class. If I wait until later, he might become self-conscious about it and refuse to share. Usually he is so excited at this point that he wants to hear it one more time anyway.

It is important for the teacher to share the *process* and not only the *product* at the end. One poet's line of thought and use of technique will inspire his/her classmates on. This early sharing helps me as a teacher give supportive criticism "on the spot" after each poet reads a work on Friday.

On this last day it is best to emphasize what is good about each "best" poem. As far as selection is concerned, the students pick the one or ones that they like best and feel most comfortable sharing. This is not always what I think is their best poem. I'll get my chance to pick poems for an anthology later. This Friday reading is an important part of the writing process.

A poem should always be read out loud. You are not done writing your poem until you hear for yourself what it sounds like. Some parts may be hard to get through. If a student stumbles over certain words, then he knows that part needs a little work.

If I know a student has a good poem, but no one else can tell because of a poor reading, then I make him start over and read it slowly and distinctly, caressing each line. I even read it for that student if he can't see how beautiful the line truly is.

As a joke, I tell him, "While you were home I wired (here I pick someone at the back of the class) Bob's desk. Under the front left hand corner of his desk there is now a button. If Bob can't hear what you're saying, then he will push that button and a trap door will open where you are standing. You'll fall through and never be heard from again."

I pull the reading student's shoulders back, point his chin so that his words are aimed at Bob in the far end of the room, not at his feet. This sounds over-bearing but if done with good humor, it works. I haven't had it back-fire yet anyway.

I ask him to read his poem as if he wrote it and knows what it's about. Once he gets over my slightly frustrating intrusions, I point out every good thing I can pick out in his poem. I ask if the class heard any metaphors or similes in the poem. Were the sounds of the words appropriate to the tone of the piece? How was the pacing, the unexpected associations?

A poet might think he wrote a sad poem and find out everyone is laughing, or he might write what he thought was a funny poem and find that the audience is deeply moved. In this way, the students can gauge if their words are doing what they intended them to.

The writers should also listen carefully to their pacing as they read. Where do they pause when reading the poem? Perhaps they should break their lines there as well to be most effective.

Class reading causes each student to stand behind her work. It forces them all to take their work seriously since they know, come Friday, they will have to read it and who knows who might be there.

As I said earlier, during the first few days I keep the door to buffoonery open wide and attempt to close it somewhat as the week progresses. Simultaneously, I try to open the door to more honest and emotionally direct poems. Nine times out of ten, the jokester who got all the laughs on Monday and Tuesday and refused to take risks thereafter, does not get any laughs on Friday. Everyone has already heard the punch line.

Meanwhile, the student who quietly made his poems burn with honesty is met with appreciative awe. Certain students in every class teach themselves a lesson here, more strongly than I could hope to.

After each poem is read, a warm round of applause is always appreciated, even if the poet knows it is forced by the teacher. Each student now feels that he has done something. Students can see their peers laugh or cry over their work. Nothing can do more to convince them that they are poets, unless it is seeing their words in print.

If there is time, I read a poem or two of my own at the end. The involved teacher also reads his/her best work for the week.

Afterward, we plan on how we are going to "publish" the best of both weeks' work: in a special booklet, the school literary magazine, the town newspaper, on a bulletin board, in local banks or businesses or maybe even read them on air at the local radio station.

I also have the teacher research what student poetry contests are coming up and how to enter them. Whether it is school-wide, county-wide, Educational Area-wide, state-wide, or on a national level--everyone loves to be recognized--teachers as well as students. Nothing keeps a good thing going like public attention. Every year my students get included in anthologies at all levels. Yours will too. Make sure you've scheduled your in-depth poetry sessions before the contests are held and not after.

9.
Formal Verse

THE VILLANELLE

Every once in a while, I come across a student with an ear for rhythm and rhyme and who wants to do something with it. I suggest books on forms and accentual syllabic patterns--but such effort fits better into a semester course of formal verse structure. Our purpose here within a two-week plan is to make the process of writing fun and exciting. Once students are hooked, a teacher can take the time and work with them in depth.

However, here are tips for what to do in one lesson to get students to write enjoyable and exciting verse.

We start out by trying to recognize the accented and unaccented syllables in a line of "Trees" by Joyce Kilmer:

```
 ∪   |    ∪|   ∪  | ∪  |
 I  think /that I /shall ne/ver see
 ∪ |    ∪  |  ∪ |  ∪ |
 a poem / as love/ly as /a tree.
```

This is an example of iambic quatrameter. The basic foot is the iam "∪/" an unaccented then an accented syllable, and there are four of them to a line. Already, this may sound a bit complex.

Listen how regular the lines are. To the modern ear it is too regular, too sing-songy: Da **da** da **da** da **da** da **da**. It no longer sounds like one friend seriously talking to another. We are more aware of the medium than the message. Modern poets must make their lines sound natural.

Beginning poets may count heavy accents, or beats, in a line. Called accentual verse, this keeping of a fairly consistent number of beats will have the effect of metered verse.

Be careful though. No inversion of word order is allowed, no archaic language. For example, in the 18th Century, Robert Southey in "The Battle of Blenheim" could say:

> It was a summer evening,
>   Old Kaspar's work was done,
> And he before his cottage door
>   Was sitting in the sun,

Now, we would have to say: He was sitting before his cottage door.

In Sonnet #1 Shakespeare could get away with:

> From fairest creatures we desire increase,
> That thereby beauty's rose might never die,
> But as the riper should by time decease
> His tender heir might bear his memory.

But we would have to say it straight out:

> We want to have children by beautiful women
> So that beauty will continue.
> So when we come to fade and die
> What we were will bloom fresh in their little faces.

Compare these to Yeats' direct and simple language in "The Song of Wandering Aengus:"

> I went out to the hazel wood,
> Because a fire was in my head,
> And cut and peeled a hazel wand,
> And hooked a berry to a thread;
> And when white moths were on the wing,
> And moth-like starts were flickering out,
> I dropped the berry in a stream
> And caught a little silver trout.

In "Adam's Curse," Yeats talks about how hard it is to make something beautiful, to write poems that seem as if they flow effortlessly even though he may have spent six hours on a line or two:

> We sat together at one summer's end,
> That beautiful mild woman, your close friend,
> And you and I, and talked of poetry.
> I said: 'A line will take us hours maybe;
> Yet if it does not seem a moment's thought,
> Our stitching and unstitching has been naught.
> Better go down upon your marrow-bones
> And scrub a kitchen pavement, or break stones
> Like an old pauper, in all kinds of weather;
> For to articulate sweet sounds together
> Is to work harder than all these, and yet
> Be thought an idler by the noisy set
> Of bankers, schoolmasters, and clergymen
> The martyrs call the world.'

As long as everyone promises to count the beats per line *and* to talk *naturally*, as if they were talking to a friend, then I show them some villanelles. This is an old French form. The lines may be of any length. There are nineteen lines divided into six stanzas -- five triplets and one quatrain -- turning on two rhymes and built on two refrains. The refrain consists of lines one and three. Once these two lines are written half the poem is done! Line one reappears as lines 6, 12 and 18; line 3 reappears as line 9, 15, and 19. Diagramed, it would look like this (A refers to rhyme #1 and B refers to rhyme #2):

VILLANELLE

Lines	Refrain and Rhymes
1	A-1--refrain
2	b
3	A-2--refrain
4	a
5	b
6	A-1--refrain
7	a
8	b
9	A-2
10	a
11	b
12	A-1--refrain
13	a
14	b
15	A-2--refrain
16	a
17	b
18	A-1--refrain
19	A-2--refrain

The overall plan is easy to see in a poem. In college, Sylvia Plath wrote "A Mad Girl's Love Song:"

A Mad Girl's Love Song

I shut my eyes and all the world drops dead;
I lift my lids and all is born again.
(I think I made you up inside my head.)

The stars go waltzing out in blue and red,
And arbitrary blackness gallops in:
I shut my eyes and all the world drops dead.

I dreamed that you bewitched me into bed
And sung me moon-struck, kissed me quite insane.
(I think I made you up inside my head.)

God topples from the sky, hell's fires fade:
Exit seraphim and Satan's men:
I shut my eyes and all the world drops dead.

I fancied you'd return the way you said,
But I grow old and I forget your name.
(I think I made you up inside my head.)

I should have loved a thunderbird instead;
At least when spring comes they roar back again.
I shut my eyes and all the world drops dead.
(I think I made you up inside my head.)
        -- Sylvia Plath

St. Francis in Ecstasy (Villanelle from a picture)

From without my needs have grown.
This fog that clouds my brain will never clear.
Even my dreams are not my own.

Religious fervor, ecstasy or agony shown?
Quiet these voices! I do not want to hear.
From without my needs have grown.

Visions of fire and death are blown
Into my mind where silence has grown dear.
Even my dreams are not my own.

In restraint my garb is sewn.
Abstinence, my only companion, is ever near.
From without my needs have grown.

Who is this God who will not be known?
What are his thoughts, his purposes, his face?
Even my dreams are not my own.

Cast in a role I would not have chosen.
Forged, molded, and made pure.
From without my needs have grown.
Even my dreams are not my own.
                    -- Margaret K. Johnson
                       (high school instructor)

Two very famous villanelles are "Do Not Go Gentle Into That Good Night" by Dylan Thomas and "The Waking" by Theodore Roethke.

While I was teaching in Council Bluffs one week, I could see that one of my students had a good ear and I showed her the preceding villanelles. She got the idea and tried one herself. She had to finish it at home though, because it was too intricate to complete in 45 minutes. The scandal of a television ministry was all over the news that week and I think the hypocrisy of some of the more public men of the cloth was on her mind.

Villanelle

I screamed inside my head and smiled again.
The zombie has a special brand of death
And angels have a different kind of sin.

The righteous ones are evil deep within;
Expound hypocrisy with every breath.
I scream inside my head and smile again.

I lick my blood from thorns and bleed once more.
Carved granite speaks of love and love of wrath.
And angels have a different kind of sin.

Clouds behind my eyes rain on my skin;
Fear like the bite of jackal-headed Seth.
I scream inside my head and smile again.

Resentment lurks behind a friendly grin;
Accursed are the liars thought to bless.
But angels have a different kind of sin.

I should know by now that Truth won't win,
And that the priests are they that need confess.
I scream inside my head and smile again,
For angels have a different kind of sin.
-- Diona Barzydlo (9th grade)

Some students will have a tough time working within a given form and still insist on writing what they call "verse." I had such a student in one of my Touring Arts Team visits. Olga made a serious attempt at a regular rhythm. At least she counted beats. She also paid attention to the appropriate sounds depending on the subject matter. She had a good natural ear and found it hard not to write in some kind of structure (although, it was usually one of her own device). We both discovered this as we went along, because she had not written much before.

Olga and her husband were long time farmers who had recently lost their farm. They had tried to bring their son into the business in the 1970's when things looked good. The

1980's brought hard times and failure. No matter how noble their efforts, they lost what they had built through generations of work. For love of their son, they had sacrificed to hand the farm on to him. Feeling the injustice and shock, she and her husband could hardly talk about farming without tears.

Olga's story touched me deeply, as I too was brought into a family farm operation under the same conditions and knew what hardship the present crisis in agriculture was causing. A whole generation of farmers was being lost, not because they were inefficient or sloppy, but because they came into it at the wrong time. If they waited twenty years, when things were a little better, it would be too late; they would have already done something with their lives to support their children.

We talked over the situation, I'm afraid, for half the class time. I recited poems which came welling up in my memory--poems which touched her concerns. Olga looked to poetry as a release. She had never written before, but felt now as if she had to, to keep her sanity. She wanted to get her mind through the sad thoughts. Her husband didn't go out much anymore and she worried about him.

I told Olga in the end to remember back earlier than the farm for a moment, to think back to the first time that she accomplished something. To make it come back to life, we did the memory assignment described earlier. She wrote, but, from habit, stuck to her old rhythm-and-rhyme ways. As she wrote along, I reminded her to be specific and natural. I helped her smooth out some of the rhythms and voilà! she had something very fine.

I asked Olga to try the last verse as a refrain, to put it between every stanza as well as the end. I told her it was so regular and so smooth, her poem sounded like a song. I could almost sing it. Since it was only the second or third poem she had ever written, she was skeptical.

At that moment, David Williams, an excellent poet and short story writer from Illinois, walked in the door looking for me. As a Touring Arts Team musician and songwriter, he just happened to have his guitar with him.

I called to him, "David, check this poem out. Don't you think it would make a nice song?"

In five minutes, he had the words set to a beautifully tender Mexican-sounding melody and we sang it back to Olga, trying to work out the harmony. Olga looked confused, and then excited, hearing it come to life before her very ears.

"Olga," I said, "come to the program tonight and bring your husband and any Mexican clothes or artifacts you can dig up."

Olga said, "I don't think my husband will come. He doesn't go anywhere. But, I'll work on him."

That night we had maracas, sombreros, guitars, piano, bongos and five part harmonies and later we even had a Tex-Mex accordion. I told everyone the story of Olga's poem and then we got the whole town to sing it and taped them all doing so. Olga had her first big hit. Her husband came and beamed with delight in her...

Gracias

Grass and trees are Texas.
Now, we're on the other side.
Cactus, prickly pear and mesquite
dot the landscape that we ride.

"No comprendo?" "Si?" or "No?"
"Muy bueno." "Por favor."
Mexico is ever calling.
"Buenos dias." "Si, Señor."

Burning sun on steaming desert.
Dusty sheep and oxen graze.
White clothed shepherds herd their charges.
I am watching in a daze.

"No comprendo?" "Si?" or "No?"
"Muy bueno." "Por favor."
Mexico is ever calling.
"Bueno dias." "Si, Señor."

In the marketplace I wonder
at the wares that are displayed:
leather crafts, carved wood and weavings
folk art, exquisite for trade.

"No comprendo?" "Si?" or "No?"
"Muy bueno." "Por favor."
Mexico is ever calling.
"Buenos dias." "Si, Señor."
                    -- Olga Borchardt

I don't know how far to take poetry as therapy. A poem
can be lousy but therapeutic, or it may be disturbingly
beautiful. Whenever I come across a student whom I feel has
the inner *need* to write, I tell him/her that that is the mark of a
true poet.

Richard Hugo, the great American poet who chaired the
Creative Writing Department at the University of Montana,

was once asked what he looked for in accepting poets into his graduate program. He said that he did not always look for the "best" poets, technically speaking. He listened to their hearts and tried to determine which of these good poets was going to write no matter. No matter what criticism--positive or negative--no matter which job they took, these true poets would write to keep sanity, whether or not they ever got published. Writing poetry is a way for their souls to breathe, their way of talking to God.

I told this to a "troubled student" I once had at the junior high level. Her parents gave first attention to their motorcycle gang and cared little what efforts she made scholastically. All her poems were depressing. Her metaphor was, "A child is a parent's worst nightmare." From there on, it went downhill emotionally. At times her words were unprintable. I wasn't sure how to criticize her at first.

Then I noticed that while everyone else was struggling with their first one or two metaphors and similes, she had done ten. Before others were done, she extended a metaphor into a whole poem. Every day she poured out power into writing.

I told her what Richard Hugo had said about souls breathing, and that I sensed, in her, the need to write.

"I hope," I told her, "that you will continue to write and develop as a writer, to listen to criticism--both good and bad-- and just keep writing."

Most of her material bristles with anger and depression now. Someday her life might change and she should be able to change her style with it and write happy poems as well. I told her that I liked her work but not because it was depressing.

"A poem doesn't have to be depressing to be good," I said.

I read her first poem, "Life Sucks," to the class. (Foul language did not seem foreign to these students, but I checked with the teacher first.) We analyzed how in the poem, everything that should have been beautiful--life, love, children--was ugly and everything that was ugly seemed beautiful--death, loneliness, depression. The whole world seemed turned upside down. This poetic inversion was the poet's way of protesting, of saying that something was wrong and should be changed. It was a cry to anyone for help.

By the end of the week, she was writing depressing but tender love poems to her dying aunt. The language had cleaned itself up. She even cleaned herself, washing and combing her hair. She wore a dress and hose to the final reading.

Her parents came to see her, surprised that they were invited to school for something other than a lecture on wayward children. The behavior change seemed dramatic. I would like to think that it held, but I know better. In one week a visiting artist cannot change a student's whole environment. If I, at least, led her to discover that she did have something inside worth developing, that she could stand up and say that she was good at something and be proud of it, then, maybe, she would have a handle to hold onto in her personal life and her scholastic endeavors. I would feel, then, like I earned my wages.

10.
Catalog Poem

THINGS TO DO

This assignment can be very effective as a sure-fire ice-breaker.

I call it a "Things to Do" poem. It is an example of cataloging. All the students have to do is to write about something they know very well. They need only make one short statement after another, telling themselves to do something. Once they've generated a long list of ideas, then they pick out the best ones and arrange them in the most effective sequence.

The catalog poem is really a variation on the old "Happiness is . . . " exercise, only with more interesting (and often more humorous) results. It is also very good for future dramatists and dramatic poets. If a poet wants to show that a character is happy, sad, bored, or frustrated, what should he make his character do? Whistle, cry, tap his fingers and look around, pace back and forth. Students enjoy making their abstract feelings concrete as you will see in some of the later student examples.

Cataloging can be an effective technique in any poem whether it is a "Things to Do" poem or not.

I am a farmer, but I'm kind of a lazy one. On rainy days, I have many farm projects that I should attend to but, often, especially when I'm in the middle of planting, I need a break. So, I write poems or books like this one. This poem takes the old saying, "All work and no play makes Jack a dull boy," and applies it to my life.

Things to Do on a Rainy Day

Listen to the incessant barking of the guineas
as they protest the rain
but are too dumb to get out of it.
Think about all the green things
that will be growing greener:
the corn, the weeds, the lawn
and the worms crawling through it.
Watch the chickens go crazy
pulling worms like stray thread from the grass.
Buy some rhubarb or a fruit tree.
Think about where you will plant it
when the dirt dries.
Weld something. If you feel like it,
re-model the coop, perhaps even, clean it.
Build a new addition to the workshop.
Think about all that you don't have to do
because the earth is too mushy.
Get ready to go to town,
but then decide not to.

Sit in the barn and watch the rain
like the dogs do.
Tap the metal seat on the tractor
to the beat of a tune
that you were sure you had forgotten.
Watch the fungus grow
on the wings of the grasshoppers
eating the hell out of your soybeans.
Change all the light bulbs in the house,
burned out or otherwise.
Fingerpaint with the children. Change the oil
in everything that has it. Kick all the tires.
Pay the bills. Enter them in the ledger.
Try to make everything balance. Think about
finding your break-even or making up a new cash-flow
   statement,
but instead, curl up before a fire and read a book.
When you're full, write a poem, maybe this one.
                    -- Michael A. Carey

A "special" student who didn't have much confidence in her work or in her other abilities wrote this first example. She had simply given up trying and sat at her desk staring at her lavender pencil. I told her she was doing a good job. Now, I wanted to know what she saw in the pencil, I wanted to see what she was dreaming about. What did she hear? If she was going to daydream, I insisted that she do it on paper.

Things to Do with a Lavender Pencil

Sit and stare at it.
Pretend you see little people
having a party. Carefully,
so as not to make them fall off,
notice how one little man
is waving at you, while
everyone else is dancing.
How everyone is wearing lavender
except for you and the little man.

Let the sweetness of the cherry punch
cool your thoughts, like a breeze
on this hot, hot day.
Feel the soft lavender flowers
near the door. Let your fingers
linger a while on the petals.
Smell the perfume
coming from the side of the room
with all the women.
Listen to the band.
It's Bon Jovi!
                    -- Laurie Griffeth (7th grade)

Things to Do When You're on the Phone

Clip your toenails.
Brush your hair.
Rub lotion on your legs.
Stare at the light bulb
until the world is full
of colored spots.
Eat a peanut butter sandwich.
Read a magazine and say, "Really?"
every five minutes.
Do exercises.
Try to figure out just who
it is you are talking to.
Then, write a letter to someone else.
Set your timer for 2 1/2 hours.
When it wakes you, say,
"Wow! That's neat!"
Listen to the T. V.
talking earnestly to an empty room.
Watch the particles of dust,
how they dance and fly
in a heaven of light.

                    -- Diane Brockshus (8th grade)

Things to Do at a Play

Sit down quickly so no one sees you with your
parents.
Read the program three or four times.
Relax when the lights go off, because your friends will
never see you.
See if your mom has any neat stuff in her purse.
Test the flashlight you find until your dad tells you
to behave.
Empty a Contac pill into your hand and try to sort the
colors.
Ask when intermission is.
Count all the people with bald heads in front of you.
As soon as intermission starts, run out and hide in the
bathroom.
Don't return until you're sure everyone is seated and
the lights are out.
Ask Dad to explain Act I quickly before the second act
starts.
Take a survey of the people around you on their
reactions to the play.
Pretend to write their answers in a notebook.
Pout when Mom tells you to be quiet.
Change seats with Dad since the man in front of you is
too big.
Return to your original seat because it was better,
after all.
Act disappointed when your parents tell you that that
was the last cultural event they'll ever take you to.
-- Susan Lyn Hagenson with
K. McCullough (high school)

What to Do in Rudd, Iowa

Go to Hoover's Hatchery and watch eggs hatch.
Count the drops of water leaking from the water tower
within one hour and calculate
how much water will be lost in one year.
Try to drive on every street in town in under three
  minutes.
See how fast you can go over the railroad tracks
without hitting your head on the roof of the car.
Try to guess the weight of the next load of corn or
beans brought into the elevator.
Watch the firemen polish the fire trucks.
Try to find ten people who pronounce Rudd
  incorrectly.
On garbage days you can see how many people use
  brown bags
and how many use black bags.
Go to the creek and count fish.
Go to the store and watch the trucks unload.
                    -- John Grosshoeme with
                        K. McCullough (high school)

11.
Editing Tips

Good poetry editing is the same as good editing of anything. The editorial skills one learns in poetry class will tide one over in any writing endeavor. Keep in mind the basic principles highlighted in the early chapters. The student should ask himself the following questions: "Is there any word I can take out without ruining the poem? Did I say the most I could in the fewest amount of words? Is there anything that should be in the poem that is missing? Did I use the right word? Am I really getting across what I want to say? Does the sound of my words reflect the feeling I want to instill in my audience? Do the lines flow from one to another? Does the rhythm work to say the words or do I stumble as I read them? Did I use a metaphor or simile or even imply one? Should I have? Did I root the experience I wanted to convey in all the senses to make it easy on my reader? Does the opening catch one's attention? Does the ending have an air of finality about it? Does the poem move predictably or is there a sense of surprise and discovery in it? Do my sentences make sense to an outsider? Are they punctuated correctly? Are the words spelled right?" (These questions, you notice, come last, but they should eventually be asked.)

How does the poem look on the page? Where does one break the lines? This, of course, is up to the individual poet, but it helps if there is a reason. If no accentual syllabic meter is used, then look for the word that will give the thought the strongest punch and break your line there. You should always be aware of what the poem looks like. Do you want a skinny

poem? If there are lots of funny, excited or nervous little
thoughts, then perhaps this would fit visually. If the thought
is heavier, more relaxed, or more ponderous, longer lines
might be in order. It will take a deeper, more controlled breath
to say them. If the poem tends to work from image to image,
then shorter lines would accentuate that. Of all the parts of
speech, a strong active verb can make the best end of a line.
The verb may make the line resonate with . . . well, whatever
information you provide around it. For example, if I said,
"Johnny got up and walked around the room," it would not be
as strong as saying:

> Johnny
> looked around the room,
> then he got up
> and walked.

Really, it doesn't mean any more than the first line did, but
it sounds like it does. So what happens if you break a line in
different spots? Does it add or detract from the poem?

Often it is effective to move, in a poem, from real, concrete
images to the abstract or metaphoric. In my poem
"Kindergarten," for instance, I started with graphic details:

> My mother wore a flat cushiony hat
> with a bouquet of plastic blossoms
> just ready to issue forth
> artificial bugs.

and ended with a metaphor:

> Above all
> I remember the muffled sobs,
> how straight my back felt in its new suit
> when I first folded my wings
> forever.

In the student letter poem I used as an example, Regina Wallace started out the same way:

> Grandma, remember when we used to bake cookies
>   together:
> peanut butter, oatmeal, chocolate chip?
> Remember how we'd steal the chips
> before they ever got in the cookies. . .

She was good and specific even to the point of naming exactly *which* cookies they baked. This specificity will lend authority to one's work. Don't say "street," say "42nd and Lexington." Then, she moved to the abstract, ending on her simile:

> And they'd melt in our mouths
> like a chocolate waterfall.

The unexpected twist of "chocolate waterfall" gives a note of finality to the piece.

One can also move from the abstract to the concrete, or become almost microscopic in detail to the point that the smallest detail takes on meaning as I tried to do in "Moving:"

> Your mother snaps the picture
> but you are not fooled
> by their confidence, their confederacy
> of smiles. You pout your face
> and shut your eyes, afraid of everything,
> not wanting to go anywhere,
> as they lead
> your reluctant little body
> snug in its fat
> new suit,
> and bow tie, and
> pink whirlybird
> hat.

No matter which way the poem moves: from concrete to abstract, or abstract to concrete, the difference, the unexpected twist of the end, will provide what is needed to punch it home.

You can also add an unexpected punch or twist by changing from liquid sounds (l, s, y, h, w, f, a, e, a(h), oo) to rough ones at the end of a poem, or from rough energetic language to a soft one. (Remember what we said about the **sound** of words in the first lesson.)

In the sonnet, "God's Grandeur," Gerard Manley Hopkins ends his poem by moving from rough, bouncing, heavily accented language to a soft energy release. The break in flow of the last line, the "ah" and "wings" all add up to a heavenly crescendo.

> And for all this, nature is never spent;
>   There lives the dearest freshness deep down things;
>   And though the last lights off the black West went
> Oh, morning, at the brown brink eastward, springs --
>   Because the Holy Ghost over the bent
>   World broods with warm breast and with ah!
>   bright wings.

As far as beginning lines are concerned just look for strong ones, ones that get you into the heart quickly.

The following is the first and second draft of a poem by a fifth grade girl in Jesup, Iowa:

Dear Grandpa (first draft)

Grandpa,
the time we spent together
was pretty like two flowers in a meadow.
Sitting by the stream
watching the baby ducks floating down the stream
like yellow roses.
Walking to the park on the green blanket of grass
as I flew down the slide like a bird.
Even when we just sat together
I felt good inside because
you're sitting by my side.
                -- Kara E. Leymaster (5th grade)

After I asked her many of the questions listed above and she changed things to suit her answers, the poem looked like this:

Dear Grandpa

We were like two pretty flowers
in a meadow by a stream
watching baby ducks
float on the water
like a garden of yellow roses.
We'd walk at the park
on the green blanket of grass.
You would always catch me
as I flew down the slide,
and cradle me in your hands
like a little bird.
Even when we just sat together
I felt good inside
because you
were right next to me.
                -- Kara E. Leymaster (5th grade)

Now, the first line jumps right into a comparison and makes the reader start asking questions to figure out what the poet means. This leads the reader on. She's rather too metaphoric at first and then becomes emotionally direct at the end. This sudden directness fills us with the love she feels.

Here is a poem that was written imagistically and yet the lines were long and prosaic. In the second draft, we zeroed in on the images and in a few quick strokes, painted them.

The Day Is Ending (first draft)

The golden yellow sun sinks behind the buildings as a huge eye closing for the night. The light pink and violet clouds as a painted eyelid seem to color the sky with peaceful goodnights. Shadows of buildings swallow up the cool water that reflects the huge eye that has almost closed all the way. I am a bug compared to this water because I am so dark and small. And now, it is the end of the day.
            -- Kay Sirdoreus (high school)

The Day Is Ending

Golden yellow
reflections on water
end a shining day.
I am a small bug
compared to the water.
Shadows swallow up the coolness
as the sun closes
its pink and violet lid
behind the darkening buildings.
            -- Kay Sirdoreus (high school)

Each poem will call out for a different set of questions. As a teacher you must ask all the ones that seem to apply and see what the student comes up with. If that doesn't do the trick, ask more. But remember, the first job of a creative writing instructor is to inspire and delight.

Acknowledgments

The author would like to thank the following publishers for giving permission to reprint the following poems:

"This Is Just To Say." William Carlos Williams: *Collected Poems 1909-1939, Vol. I.* Copyright © 1938 by New Directions Publishing Corporation. Reprinted by permission of New Directions Publishing Corporation.

"Mad Girl's Love Song" by Sylvia Plath. Courtesy *Mademoiselle.* Copyright © 1953 by the Conde Nast Publications Inc.

Certain of Michael Carey's poems first appeared in the following magazines and journals:

"Graveside: December 1981" in *Corridors*

"Kindergarten" in *Mr. Cogito*

"Early American Small Print Wallpaper" in *Portland Review*

"Moving" in *New Jersey Poetry Journal*

The cataloging exercise in Chapter 10 was given to the author by Bill Broz, a high school writing instructor in Fairfield, Iowa. Bill was given the idea by the Iowa City poet, Ken McCullough, who picked it up from the poems of the Pulitzer Prize-winning poet, Gary Snyder.

Thanks to the students who gave their consent for me to include their poems in this book. Those poems are the taste that proves the pudding good.

Thanks also to the Iowa, Missouri, and Nebraska Arts Councils, and KJG Farms, Inc., for their support; Kelly, Helen, Maeve, and Andrew for their love and patience; and Duane Hutchinson whose idea it all was.